AF545106

Our Plant Friends and Foes

REDWOOD TREES

Our Plant Friends and Foes

By

WILLIAM ATHERTON DuPUY

Introduction by

WILLIAM A. TAYLOR

DOVER PUBLICATIONS, INC., NEW YORK

Published in Canada by General Publishing Company, Ltd., 30 Lesmill Road, Don Mills, Toronto, Ontario.
Published in the United Kingdom by Constable and Company, Ltd., 10 Orange Street, London WC 2.

This Dover edition, first published in 1969, is an unabridged republication of the text of the revised edition of the work originally published by The John C. Winston Company in 1930. The half-tone illustrations on the following pages, selected for this Dover edition and replacing those which appeared in the original edition, were supplied courtesy the United States Department of Agriculture: frontispiece, 9, 12, 26, 35, 51, 59, 62, 65, 68, 72, 76, 86, 88, 92, 95, 99, 113, 115, 116, 120, 125, 126, 130, 134, 146, 156, 159, 161, 163, 171, 181, 184, 186, 189, 193, 195, 202, 206, 217, 222, 226, 234, 262, 267, 272, 275.

Standard Book Number: 486-22272-1
Library of Congress Catalog Card Number: 72-78060

Manufactured in the United States of America
Dover Publications, Inc.
180 Varick Street
New York, N.Y. 10014

PREFACE

For many generations men have sought for the secrets of the plant world and written them into books. Their enthusiasm has been that of the zealot; their industry has put the beaver and the busy bee to shame. The facts that have been gleaned are so many that it is beyond the possibilities of any man to learn them all. And yet the field of botany, as a science, is quite inadequately explored. There is still much lack of agreement as to its organization and nomenclature.

These men of science have produced books that quite well serve the purpose of that individual who is to devote his life to botany. Such a man masters the technical terms of the science and his exceptional interest carries him through seas of detail. But when the casual reader turns to botany with no more than a normal curiosity to know something of the world about him, he is likely to find himself quite overwhelmed. The literature of the plant world has not been written for him but for the technician. For his use it requires a liberal and understanding translation, and botany seems to have received rather less of this treatment than other branches of natural history.

I have tried to prepare a book which will be easy for anybody to read, and which might even provide entertainment for the normal, nontechnical individual. I have proceeded on the theory that few persons want to become botanists, but that many would be interested in knowing more of the living world about them. There is the fact, for example, that every green leaf that turns its face to the sun is a sugar factory busily at work. All growth in this world, animal or vegetable, is based on the leaf that makes sugar in the sun. It is one of the world's great fundamental facts, but it is quite unknown to all save a chosen few. It has remained unknown because the books that have discussed it have been difficult to read.

The scientist, working through the years on his specialty, becomes quite absorbed in it. The meticulous details of it become vital to him. Its terminology is a part of his everyday vocabulary. His thought is of his science and not of the reader. He is likely to go further into detail than the unscientific reader will follow. He is likely to use terms that are not understood.

The viewpoint of the writer for general publication must be quite different. He is thinking all the time of the reader. He must hold the attention of this casual reader who will turn the page the moment that he is bored. What he writes must therefore be easy to read. He must so dress his facts that they are pleasing to the beholder, that they will induce him to follow from paragraph to paragraph, from page to page. The reader will follow only what most interests him in the theme before him, in the magazine at his elbow, or in the book on his shelf. The book which carries its message to the casual reader must successfully meet this competition.

This book has not been written for the botanist. It is intended for the normal and wholesome intelligence of the fourteen-year-old boy; for the casual perusal of the young woman who grows flowers in her garden and goes tramping in the woods; and as fireside reading for the elderly couple who find keen enjoyment in reading. Its intention is not to add greatly to the training of botanists, though it may arouse in many a first interest in that subject which may lead to more ambitious explorations. It is the hope of the author that those who read will get some insight into the simple phenomena of the plants that grow all about them.

And what a world of interest there is for him who has been given the key of understanding! How enjoyable it is to trace the relationship among the plants round about us! It is as easy to see that the locust tree, the wistaria vine, and the clover of the fields are cousins, as it is to note a relationship between the Chinese and the Japanese. The sweet-potato vine and the morning-glory used to be the same, but they have grown apart. Watermelons are gourds; the apple tree is a rosebush grown large; sugar cane is a grass; the daisy is one of man's worst enemies.

Although I have tried to make many facts of the plant world readily available to the casual reader, I have endeavored at the same time to hold them to a strict scientific accuracy. The great scientific bureaus of the Federal Government have extended every facility to me in the preparation of this volume. Among these has been the Bureau of Plant Industry of the Department of Agriculture, which employs more men of science than does any other single agency in the world. Nowhere else has there ever been built up such a repository of information on plants as in this government bureau.

Dr. William A. Taylor, its chief, has helped me throughout the building of this book. When it was finished, he read the copy on it to insure its scientific accuracy. Having read it himself, he then referred each chapter to the specialist under him who knows most about the particular plants treated. Thus the facts have been checked and corrected by two and sometimes three scientists before going to press.

Dr. Taylor did me the honor to write an introduction to the book, for which I express my gratitude.

WILLIAM ATHERTON DU PUY

CONTENTS

ILLUSTRATIONS

INTRODUCTION

One reason that plants are so little understood is that they are so common. They are everywhere about us—under our feet when we walk on the grass, over our heads when we stroll under the trees, and in the air we breathe, although we cannot see them. "All flesh is grass" is a truism which, if fully realized, would compel us to know plants better and to appreciate more highly the part they play in this fragment of the universe which we call the world. It would force us to realize what we often overlook, that plants constitute the essential connecting bond between man and Mother Earth.

Plants are not the simple, inert things that they may appear to be to one who wanders casually among them. Often the simplest of them may have marvelous characteristics, combining in a small space rare beauty and high usefulness. Many of them have played important parts in man's slow climb from his primitive state. They have risen with him from their original forms, as he has acquired better understanding of them and developed skill in growing and utilizing them.

Many books have been written about plants, and many more are needed. Most of these doubtless should record with exactness new discoveries or describe better methods of growing, handling, and utilizing them and their products. The author of this little volume, however, has a different objective. He has endeavored to bring together certain interesting facts, many of them long known to plant growers and to students, and to present them in the everyday language which the ordinary person may understand. He has not attempted to produce a technical manual but rather, through stimulation of our interest, to help us to get acquainted with some important plants which we need to know more intimately. He has consulted many specialists in different fields of plant research in his sifting of the mass of material which he accumulated. If, in bringing some of the existing gaps between the known facts in the prehistoric relationships of plants and man, he has drawn on the resources of an alert constructive imagination, that does not lessen the usefulness of the book. It should serve a worth-while educational purpose by bringing home to a large class of readers some general information about plants which is both interesting and instructive.

William A. Taylor
Chief of the Bureau of Plant Industry
Department of Agriculture

ACKNOWLEDGMENT

Grateful acknowledgment is made by the author and publishers to the United States Department of Agriculture for its courtesy in supplying photographs for use in this book.

Our Plant Friends and Foes

CHAPTER I

THE APPLE AND ITS COUSINS

WHEN the human race was young, its Aryan branch from which Western peoples sprang, dwelt about the shores of the Caspian Sea, in southwest Asia. These people found a fruit of the woods that was sweet to them and took it unto themselves.

Thousands of years later, the Anglo-Saxons in western Europe fitted a word to this fruit. Because they did so, Americans, who eat more of it than all the rest of the world combined, talk every day from coast to coast of apples.

Today a wild apple, the crab apple, is to be found growing in the colder parts of many lands around the world. These apples are tart and bitter and not very good to eat. But along the Caucasus foothills west of the Caspian Sea there are wild apples that are sweet. It was doubtless these that began to be planted about the villages of the Aryans when they made their early attempts at agriculture.

Scientific students of plants today know that one of the best ways to improve them is by selecting the seeds of the most perfect specimens in each generation and by planting them for the new crop. For example, a long time ago the Chinese noticed that an occasional daisy in the field was bigger and better than its fellows. They planted the seeds of these superior daisies. Among the new plants there might be certain ones that were bigger and better even than the selected parent. These in turn were planted for a new crop. In the end the Chinese developed the chrysanthemum from the daisy.

The early Aryans did not know this law of selection, but it was natural that they should plant the seeds of the apples that were sweet to them. Those which they liked best were carried far from the forests in which they grew and were planted. When these peoples started on their migrations, they carried with them the seeds of their best apples. They might move a thousand miles to the west and live there for generations, growing apples all the time. Then they might make another migration, taking their favorite seeds with them. Thus were sweet apples bred by a natural selection and spread well over Europe even before modern civilization began.

When the new world came in for settlement, another chapter in apple history was written. The oldest apple orchard in the United States was planted by Franciscan fathers at a mission which they founded among the Indians near what is now the town of Manzano, in central New Mexico. It is believed to have been started in 1636, which makes it about 300 years old. The trees of it are still growing. Knotted with age, they stand in little clusters. This indicates that the first tops of these trees ran their courses, died down, and a new cluster of plants sprang up from around their roots. But there they are, the first apple heritage of the nation, still living after three centuries and still bearing fruit.

French Jesuit priests carried apples to Canada and the Northwest. They also came to Massachusetts and to Virginia with the early settlers. They followed those settlers in their wanderings. The final classic of the apple was written into our history by one Jonathan Chapman and has come down to us as a pioneer legend through a hundred years of Ohio life as "Johnny Appleseed."

On the bank of Licking Creek, Ohio, then a nearly trackless wilderness, in the year 1801, a ragged young man with a horse laden with a strange burden paused, took from the store he carried, and planted seeds. He went on, but, as the years passed, apple trees sprang up here and bore fruit. Thus was written the first chapter in the story of Johnny Appleseed.

Five years later the record shows him pushing two canoes spliced together up the Black Fork of the Mohican, farther into the wild country. These canoes were laden with the same strange burden as the horse of the earlier journey—apple seeds.

Again the stranger would appear on foot with bags on his back filled with this same burden. Each time he had traveled tediously all the way back to the cider presses of Pennsylvania, where apple seeds were abundant and free. Always he plunged into the wilderness and went on and on, planting his apple seeds. Wherever a woodsman had started a modest clearing in the forest, there Johnny Appleseed sowed these germs of the orchards of the future, and left instructions about transplanting and cultivating them. Wherever he found an Indian village, there he planted apple trees and told the red men about their fruit. Even in the great open stretches, where his vision of the future told him that settlers would come some day, he planted seeds that fruit might be there to welcome them. Somehow he felt that these settlers, living largely on "hog and hominy," would suffer from scurvy just as sailor men used to suffer on long voyages for lack of fruit acids in their diet.

As the years passed, all the white men and red men of this region came to know and reverence Johnny Appleseed. A man of education was he, and of fervent religious spirit. He had chosen for himself a life which he thought was that of the "primitive Christian" as set down in the Bible. Never during those years of frontier wandering did he carry a gun or do violence to man or beast.

At first he wore the cast-off rags of the settlers, but later he adopted as his unchanging costume a coffee sack with slits for head and arms and a cap which he himself had made of pasteboard. He went barefoot even late into the winter. He would accept no more hospitality than the privilege of lying on the floor before a settler's fire where, by the flickering light, it was his habit to read from his Bible and other religious books.

Johnny Appleseed died on such a settler's floor after forty-six years of this strange orchard planting. His wandering was not without its heroic moments, as, for example, when he hurried from settlement to settlement giving warning of the advance of the Indian allies of the British during the trying years of the War of 1812. The heritage that he left through much suffering was countless apple trees that blossomed gloriously in the spring. They ripened their autumn treasures for the children of the drear frontier. This task, well done, challenges the centuries to produce a better example of service to one's fellows.

And having traveled this long way, it comes to pass that there is today a producing apple tree in the United States for every man, woman, and child beneath the flag. The apple is the greatest of American fruit crops. The value of the apple crop, year by year, is greater than that of peaches and grapes combined, and they rank next it. The bulk of the crop is nearly that of all the other fruit crops combined. The apple crop is, in fact, a most overwhelming thing. Trainloads and shiploads of apples come out of Canada, whose vigorous climate they love. Gnarled trees, a century old, stud New England from end to end. Western New York has always claimed the apple for its own. In the piedmont regions of Virginia it matures magnificently. Ohio, Michigan, and Wisconsin group it about their comfortable farm homes. The Ozark Mountains invite it farther to the south. Colorado gives whole irrigated valleys over to it. The states of Washington and Oregon have built a magnificent industry on preparing its choicest specimens for the markets of the world. It knows the markets of every city, town, and hamlet in the nation. It is the universal fruit, the king of all the fruit crops of the world.

When one comes to think of the apple tree from the standpoint of the great vegetable kingdom, to wonder what is the particular niche into which it fits, to look about for its relatives, one is likely to hit upon a number of surprises. There are families in plants, of course, just as there are in human beings. One recognizes a Chinese as belonging to the Mongolian race and a Negro as belonging to the Ethiopian race. They are both men, but each has his peculiarities by which he can be classified and put into a particular group.

It is the same with plants. The grass family has the peculiarity of joints. The members of the bean family put up their seeds in pods. Members of the fern group have one appearance and of the pine group another. In each there are family characteristics which set the group apart.

THE ROSE AND APPLE LEAF ARE MUCH ALIKE

One would not be likely to guess the group to which the apple belongs. It is a member of the rose family. As a matter of fact, the apple tree is but a rosebush grown great. One might never have thought of it as a rose, but once the idea is planted, the fact begins to become quite plain. To be sure, the leaves of the two plants are similar. Then, if the flower of the apple is compared with that of the wild rose, they are found to be much alike. The cultivated rose, of course, has been bred through selection, as was the chrysanthemum, and is quite different from the wild rose from which it came.

An examination of the rosebush shows that it actually bears an apple. After the bloom has gone, it forms a seed pod which is round, smooth, glossy, and often highly colored. It is for all the world like a tiny apple. The seeds are put up inside much as they are in an apple. In the case of the apple, the seed pod has been padded out with much meat. This is a habit which the apple developed as it grew to be different from the rose. The crab apple, which is practically the wild apple, has not so much meat about its seeds as has the cultivated apple. In fact, it is about as near the rose apple as it is to the cultivated apple.

The pear, of course, belongs in this family group. So does the peach, the plum, the quince, the cherry—most of the important fruits of the orchard. The leaves and the flowers of all these are of the same type as those of the wild rose.

There is another large group that has developed from the rosebush in another direction, but which, come to think of it, has family traits that show close relationship. These are the berries. The blackberry vine, for example, is a rosebush not so very different from the wild rose. Its flower and its leaves are much the same. It has come to put up its seeds in a different kind of package. It has developed a berry. It did this as a temptation to the birds. Its berry is attractive to the birds, and they come to eat it. They carry it away and drop it in new places. In this way does the blackberry vine find new homes. It has gone to all this trouble of developing berries which the birds like just to get its seeds scattered about.

The raspberries are members of the rose family. So are the strawberries. Thus it comes about that the modest little strawberry clinging to the ground belongs to the same family as the lofty peach tree with its wagon load of fruit ready for the cannery.

A sturdy plant person is this apple tree. Stocky and well set up, it stands there on the hillside. Its trunk with age has formed the habit of building slabs of bark that curl up around the edges and in the end slough off. Its branches push themselves out in a most aggressive manner. There are many elbows in them, angular and strong. They seem to defy the elements. They are indifferent to the gustiest of winds that blow. The snows of winter may pile in their crotches as they please. These apple trees are here to stay, and who will dispute their right?

In the wild state the apple tree branches near the ground and often thereafter. It is, however, a tree and not a shrub. The difference between these two, it should be remembered, marks two great divisions in the plant world. The shrub branches at or beneath the ground and sends up many stalks. The tree rises from the earth on a single trunk and does its branching after it has started growing. This apple bearer is a tree, although it has a tendency to branch out close to the ground and rarely to grow very high.

Spring, with its wealth of tender leaves and its bountiful bouquet of pink blossoms, soon covers the rough winter apple-tree form and converts it into a thing of glory. Summer brings its dense foliage and sprays of growing fruit. Through the centuries the sturdy limbs of apple trees have borne the swings of children, and song and story have paid their tribute to the happy days of which they were a part. Few trees, if any, in the United

States, have figured more intimately in the lives of passing generations.

The apple tree is a child of the north. It likes the rugged climate of Maine and Canada. It roots deep into the soil and holds its place for a hundred, two hundred years. Certain varieties of it have been grown

AN APPLE ORCHARD

farther south for a long time and have adapted themselves to warmer climates. But they object to being carried into the land of the oranges.

If a northern apple tree is planted in Florida, for example, it suffers intensely. It is like a human being with nervous prostration. In the north it has been accustomed to its long sleep through the winter. Yet it cannot sleep unless the weather turns cold. It does not understand this failure of the cold to arrive. It does not shed its leaves; yet this being an evergreen does not suit it. It puts forth flowers at odd times. It rarely ripens fruit and if it does, that fruit has lost its vigor. It is a sickly sort of fruit that decays quickly. This tortured son of the north lives miserably for a few years in the southland and then dies of exhaustion.

But farther north apple trees surround millions of the homes of people on the upper edge of the temperate zone. When springtime comes, new life surges into the crooked apple-tree limbs. Almost overnight there is a transformation. The rose and white mingle with spring's young green, and the bees come to drone at their honey gathering. The falling petals shower in the breeze and drift into banks by the fence corners. Then comes summer with its checkered light and shade, the abundant green above sifted through with blue and gold drowsing beneath the trees. Then harvest time hangs scarlet apples among the yellowing leaves—winesaps and pippins, blood red and gold. And on winter evenings they lead to much munching before the fire. They travel far away to city homes, and are likely to be found in the lunches of children who go to school. Far radiating and joyful is the spread of this master fruit.

CHAPTER II

THE CHERRY BRANCH OF THE ROSE FAMILY

CHERRIES, like apples, are members of the rose family. They have the same sort of leaves, the same sort of blossoms, and certain points of similarity in their fruit.

It has been shown that the rose and the apple put up their seeds in the same sort of package, but that the apple acquired the habit of packing meat that was good to eat about its seeds. It did this so that boys and animals would carry the apples away, eat them, and scatter the seed far and wide. It was because of this meat around its seeds that the apple was planted all over the world.

Cherries likewise bribe animals to carry them away, that their seeds may be dropped in new places and start new fruit colonies. It is for this that the peaches, the plums, and all the rest of them make themselves good to eat. It is strange that the almond is a member of this same group, but has developed into a nut instead of a fruit. At some time its pit was found to be good to eat. This bribed animals to carry the pit away instead of the flesh of the almond. Thus it became an almond instead of a peach, not seeming very much at home in its own family circle.

Although the cherry and the apple both belong to the rose family, they differ in the sort of package in which they put up their seeds. The apple has a group of seeds in its core while the cherry has a single seed put away in a stone. This difference in the seeds they produce shows that, while both are members of the rose family, they are not closely related. The apple and the pear, for example, are closer kin than the apple and the cherry.

HARVESTING TART RED CHERRIES

Both pack their seeds in the same way. In the same way the cherry and the peach are closer kin than the cherry and the apple. Both inclose their seeds in stones. The apple and the pear are about as closely related as are first cousins among human beings, while the apple and the cherry may be thought of as second cousins.

Botanists call the fruits that put up their seeds as does the apple "pomes." In French an apple is a "pomme." Such fruits are members of the pome branch of the rose family. Scientists call those that put up their fruit as does the cherry "drupes." They are members of the drupe branch of the rose family. They are the stone fruits. They include cherries, plums, peaches, apricots, nectarines, almonds, and others. Their relationship to each other is like that of first cousins.

Taking the cherries by themselves, it is easy to show

CHERRIES READY FOR MARKET

an even closer relationship. There are two principal kinds of cherries known to man—the sour cherry and the sweet cherry. The big cherries sold in markets and eaten raw are of the sweet variety, while those used for canning and sold for making pies are sour cherries. Each is better than the other for the purpose which it serves.

The trees on which these two kinds of cherries grow differ in appearance. The sweet cherry tree grows big and tall. The sour cherry tree is low and bushy, more nearly the size of a peach tree. Yet they are closely alike in leaves, blossoms, general characteristics of the fruit, and the stone pits which contain the seed. They are more closely related to each other than is either of them to the peach, the plum, or the apricot. They are brothers and sisters.

The cherry, like most of the orchard fruits, came with the Aryans out of Asia. Seventy years before Christ, Lucullus, a Roman general, returning from a campaign in the East, brought cherry seeds to the city of seven hills. When the Romans invaded what is now England, 120 years later, they took cherries with them. Cherries have been scattered all over Europe. They have come to America. The big, sweet cherry has found its favorite home on the slopes of the Sierra Nevada Mountains. Yet in Europe it has come into a prettier usefulness. The sweet cherry tree grows to large size and is a very satisfactory shade tree. In many communities in Europe these trees border the public roads for scores of miles and produce luscious fruit in abundance for the whole countryside.

The cherry, like all orchard fruits, is a flowering plant. This means that it is also one of the plants which depend for existence on the help of bees and other insects. Without the aid of these insects there would be no cherry trees. Neither would there be apple trees, peach trees, nor any other of the ordinary fruits. The help of insects, chiefly bees, in growing those fruits that are the favorites of mankind is one of the outstanding miracles of Nature, one of the best examples of helpfulness between the animal and the vegetable kingdoms.

Whoever has played with buttercups or daisies or any other of the common blossoms has noticed the fine dust in the hearts of the flower. This dust is called *pollen.* Few people ever think of attaching any importance to it, but, as a matter of fact, it is one of the most important substances in the plant world.

The most important thing that the plant has to do is to grow seeds. If it does not do this, its race will die out. Everywhere in Nature careful attention is given to the new generation.

The plant takes great care in producing its seeds. The appearance of the blossom is the first step in seed making. Every blossom contains pollen. Unless the seed-forming organ of a flower is dusted with pollen, no seeds will be developed. Some flowers are satisfied with the pollen which they themselves produce, but many require pollen from other flowers. Thus it is shown that the very life of all flowering plants which help feed the human race depends on pollen and must find a way to carry it from one flower to another.

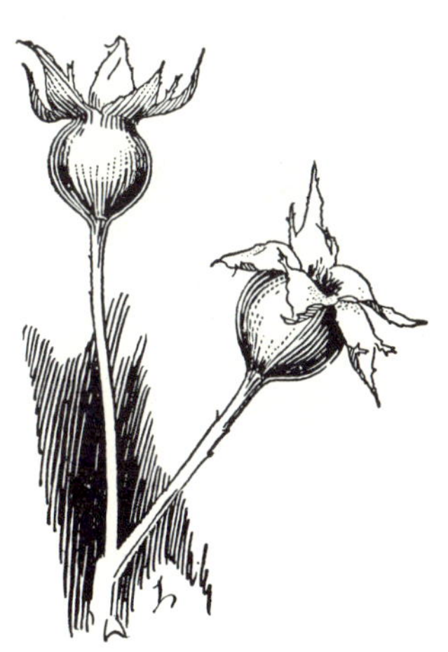

THE ROSEBUSH HAS AN APPLE OF ITS OWN

For some plants, such as the grasses, the wind carries the pollen. Some flowers produce their own pollen. Many plants, however, depend on insects to bring the pollen to them. Plants make great efforts to induce insects to bring pollen to them from other plants. If the insects should go on a strike in the spring, we would have no fruit that summer. But insects will not go on a strike because they know that they would starve if they did, since they get their living from these same flowers.

The bee is the greatest of pollen carriers. It has a fuzzy sort of head to which the pollen sticks. When it crowds its head down a cherry blossom, a great many particles of pollen are sure to stick to it. Then, when it goes to the next flower and thrusts its head deep into it, some of these pollen particles are sure to be shaken off. These particles of pollen fertilize that flower. They cause it to bear fruit and seed. On this exchange of pollen depends the very existence of flowering plants.

INSECTS CARRY POLLEN FROM ONE FLOWER TO ANOTHER

When one sees the flowers blooming so beautifully in the spring, he is not likely to realize that the plants on which they grow have a very practical reason for making the blossoms beautiful. The chief purpose of beauty in flowers is to attract insects to them so that they will carry pollen to other plants. All the beauty of the blossoming world is put on, not to gratify man, but to attract bees and other insects that may be buzzing around them.

Odors are given to flowers to attract or drive off insects. Insects have a very delicate sense of smell. On the other hand, their sense of sight is very poor. They can see objects only four or five feet away. The experiment has been tried of taking a butterfly half a mile away from its mate which was held captive and then turning him loose. He returned, guided by his keen sense of smell. Often through the sense of smell, flowers induce insects to come near them.

But this is not the end of the efforts which flowers make to get the insects to visit them. The final offering is actual food. Flowers make nectar, or honey, which they place deep in their cups. This nectar is the favorite food of many insects. They live on it through the season of their spring and summer activities. Bees, especially, carry it home to feed to their young or store it in their hives for food during the winter.

This honey is the actual pay to the insect for carrying pollen from one flower to another. There are many strange facts about the way in which this work is done. For example, the flower of red clover has a cup that is so deep that the bill of the ordinary bee cannot reach to the bottom of it. Only the bumblebee can reach the honey in red clover blossoms. It often happens that, when red clover seed is planted in a country where there are no bumblebees, the clover will make no seed and consequently the crop will fail. When a red clover crop fails, the scientist generally knows that bumblebees must be brought into that country. Thus it has happened that bumblebees have been shipped all over the world to make the clover produce seed.

There are certain plants that bloom at night and close up their blossoms during the day. They do this for very strange reasons which have to do with the activities of insects that are night workers. Among these are certain moths that feed on the nectar of flowers. It is to these moths that the night-blooming flowers appeal. In the dark they make their appeal to the insects through their very strong odors. The cloying odor of such flowers as that of the night-blooming cereus is well known.

Whoever thought that the morning-glory, in coming out so early and "putting up its shutters" when the sun was well on its journey, was fighting the battle for very existence over this same task of making its seed through the help of insects! The morning-glory, trailing there on the ground and in olden times blooming in the daytime, found that it had got itself into trouble. The ant, which is a cousin of the bee, also likes honey. That insect found out that there was honey in the morning-glory cup and, being a bold and energetic sort of person, walked right in and helped itself. But the ant had no fuzz on its head that would carry pollen. In fact, its dome was smooth as glass, and pollen slipped right off. When it reached the next flower, it had no pollen. It was merely robbing the flower of honey that might otherwise have been given to the bee which would bring this vital spark of plant life.

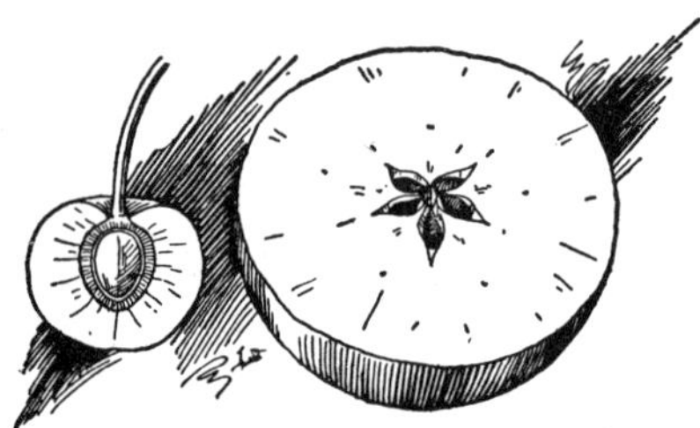

THE CHERRY AND THE APPLE, THOUGH COUSINS, PUT UP THEIR SEEDS IN DIFFERENT WAYS

So the morning-glory worked out a scheme for opening its flower to the bees and closing it to the ants. It studied the working hours of these two insects. It found that the bee, buzzing on busy wings, was out bright and early. It found, on the other hand, that the ant, having to plod along on foot, could not get around very well until the dew was off the grass. There were some two hours in the morning when this flower might offer its bribe to the bees without the ants giving it any trouble. The flower worked out a scheme of opening shop during those two hours and putting up the shutters by the time the dew was off the grass. Thus it manages to get along quite nicely.

The plant world feeds the innumerable insects that are honey eaters. The insects, on the other hand, render a service that is beyond price to the plants. It is the old game of give and take. Man stands on the side lines, harvests vast quantities of delicious fruit and profits thereby, despite the fact that he takes no part in these vital processes of Nature.

The wild brothers to the orchard cherry trees are natives to America. Although their fruit is rarely tempting, the wood is highly prized for making cabinet furniture of a high sheen and polish. There are also ornamental varieties of the cherry that are used in many countries for the beauty of their blossoms alone. In Japan, the Cherry Blossom festival is a time of great rejoicing. Every spring the beauty of the Japanese cherry trees transplanted along the Potomac River in Washington, D. C., is a target for visitors from all over the country. Thus the cherry in all its forms provides outstanding services for man.

Chapter III

THE BEAN FAMILY

SO STRANGE are the relationships in the vegetable kingdom that one finds that the clover of the meadow, cropped by the patient cow, the wistaria vine that runs over its trellis and beautifies the spring, and the locust tree which lifts its top to the sky, are all blood cousins.

An examination will show that each has a bean in which it packs its seeds for future crops and that this bean is the mark of relationship. The string bean of the dinner table may be cited as a most familiar representative of such a crop. The botanist is likely to classify these bean bearers as members of the *pulse* family; or he may designate them as *legumes*. If one will study the formation of the sweet-pea blossom, he will find a scheme of petal arrangement that runs through the family. Likewise, he is likely to find an arrangement of leaves that marks the bean bearers. The clover, for example, has a leaf at the end of the stem and two more opposite each other lower down. The locust tree has this same arrangement, except that it adds many more leaflets

CLOVER LEAVES AND THOSE OF THE LOCUST TREE BEAR FAMILY LIKENESSES

down the stem. Many of the members of this family have this locust-like, multiplied leaf.

In tropical jungles there are vines on which beans are developed that are three feet long and four inches wide. They are members of this family. The peanut of commerce grows on a plant with pealike leaf and bloom. After blossoming the peanut plant does a strange thing. It thrusts the tips of these flowering branches into the ground and its seeds develop there, ready planted for the next year.

The peanut is a bean. Man has learned to dig up its underground pods and sell them in bags at baseball games. The wistaria vine is a bean that has developed in a different way. The hardy mesquite tree of the deserts of America's Southwest is a bean bearer. So is the coffee tree of Kentucky with its pods a foot long. So also is that choice, clover-like plant often baled and sold for fodder, the alfalfa of the fields, which is becoming a most popular crop. That ornamental plant, the Judas tree, and the acacia of the East are also bean bearers.

The members of this bean group are noted for the strange movements to which their leaves are given. The three leaflets of the clover stem, for example, fold themselves together like hands in prayer and go to sleep at nighttime. The leaflets of the acacia fold themselves tightly along their stems after sunset. Stranger still is the action of the sensitive plant which is a cousin to the locust. A leaf stem with its many leaflets may be standing bolt upright. If it is touched, however, it wilts instantly. Both stem and leaves droop most sadly. No other plant is so responsive to mere touch. The

THE PEANUT IS A BEAN

conduct of the telegraph plant is even stranger. It has one large leaf at the end of its stem and two small ones lower down. These smaller leaves work constantly, assuming one position after another, as might a boy scout wigwagging a message. At night the big leaf at the end goes to sleep and hangs at rest. The little leaves never stop. They go on and on throughout the night.

Anyone interested in the bean group will have little trouble in recognizing members of that group wherever they are found. The bean itself, the blossom, the arrangement of leaves, is everywhere the same so far as basic patterns are concerned. The bean quality is hard to find in the seed pod of the clover, but it is none the less there. It is more easily recognized in alfalfa, despite the fact that the bean curls itself into a tight little knot.

Rich indeed is the contribution which this family makes to the welfare of mankind. The value of clover and of alfalfa as forage and hay crops is easily appreciated. They follow man and his live stock around the world and contribute to their well-being. Peas and beans are so closely related that it is hard to tell where one group ends and the other begins. The beans furnish prime foodstuffs for man and beast. They have fed millions of people down through the centuries. They furnish a rich, heavy food, full of proteins, the substance that gives food values to meats. Beans are Nature's vegetable substitute for meats. Any person who has no meat to eat may find an excellent substitute in a pot of beans. Many millions of people in many parts of the world do this every day.

When the world was young, the bean was not widely scattered. It has none of the tricks of some plants for getting its seed borne far away that it may start new colonies. The thistle puts sails on its seeds so that they may ride the wind. The cocklebur sticks in the tail of a horse, to be released, probably months later, at some distant spot. But the bean drops beneath the bush that bears it and is likely to stop near home. In the beginning, there were beans only in Asia, probably somewhere near the south end of the Caspian Sea, and in equally small areas in America. They did not scatter far until the human race began to develop and found in them a quite satisfactory food. Then they were carried east and west and planted all over the world. In America the Indians were growing them in their corn fields when the white man came. Now they are used everywhere.

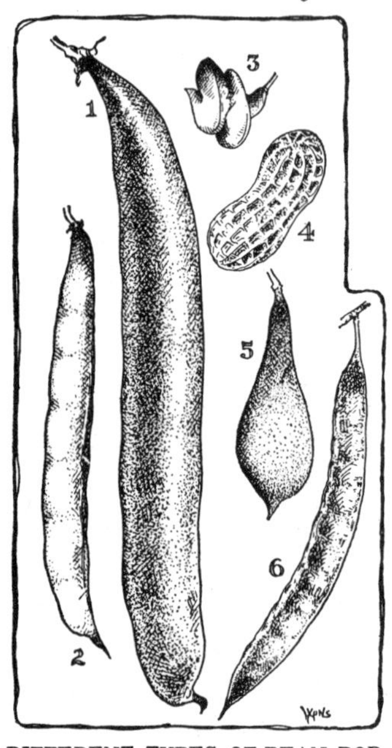

DIFFERENT TYPES OF BEAN POD
1. Broad bean. 2. Wax bean. 3. Alfalfa. 4. Peanut. 5. Wistaria. 6. Honey Locust.

The broad bean of Europe is called the *bean of history*. Its vine furnished the ladder for Jack-and-the-beanstalk fame. Its seeds were eaten by the lake dwellers of Switzerland, who were the earliest people of Europe. It has been found in the tombs of the Pharaohs. The Greeks knew it before the time when they used copper pots as money in their early market transactions. Originally it was a tropical plant, but man crowded it farther and farther into the north.

Wherever people are poor, beans are most likely to be cultivated. They are eaten much in Europe. In Mexico the native American bean, called the *frijole*, probably the best bean for food of them all, is the staff of life of the common people. Soy beans grow in China and Manchuria, where they compete with rice as a good and nourishing food. Green peas, string beans, kidney beans, and lima beans are sold in all markets of the United States.

The use of beans as food is more highly developed in China than elsewhere. There they are cooked and prepared in such a way that a liquid not unlike milk results. Here again is the likeness to animal fats shown. From this milk the Chinese make cheeses that have as many odors and flavors as do the cheeses that Europeans and Americans make from cows' milk. These Chinese cheeses may be bought in most towns or cities in America where Chinese merchants are to be found. If it ever comes to pass that America should be densely populated and poor, people will surely turn to beans for their food.

Recently in the United States an example was given of the manner in which a crop such as beans crowds gradually into new territory. In Florida a tropical vine known as the velvet bean was being grown for live stock or for fertilizer. It grew so rapidly and so thickly that people planted it around the porches of their houses for shade. This bean was grown in North Carolina for the same purpose. However, in North Carolina it would not produce bean pods, because the summer was not long enough for it to complete the cycle of its natural life and mature its seed. So the people of North Carolina had to send to Florida each year for new seed to plant around their porches.

Finally, however, someone noticed that a single plant of this velvet bean had produced pods and seeds. This observer was wise enough to know that here was a plant which was different from others of its kind. This velvet bean had matured as far north as North Carolina. Its

SOY BEANS IN A CONTOURED FIELD

seeds were planted and grown. It was the parent of a new race of velvet beans that now grow through a tier of states where none of its kind had grown before. It gave to North Carolina and the states of the same latitude a new crop that now yields them millions a year. It has shown us how useful crops may be pushed into a new territory.

The lowly bean surely has done its share of the work of

the world by providing a cheap and wholesome food for many millions of people. But members of the bean family do a much more important thing than this. They perform one of the miracles of Nature by adding to the richness of the soils of the world and therefore to the abundance of all crops.

Science tells us that nitrogen is one of the most abundant of elements. About eighty per cent of the air we breathe is nitrogen. The air forms a covering for the earth about fifty miles in thickness. Consequently there is no substance so plentiful as nitrogen. Despite this, many plants of the world are suffering from lack of nitrogen. Vast areas of them starve to death every year from lack of this nitrogen with which they are surrounded, because it is not in proper form for their use. The members of the bean group have a way all their own of taking the nitrogen from the air and of putting it into the ground where all plants can use it as food. Their greatest purpose is served in this handling of nitrogen. It is a service to all plant life. It is doubtful if any other group of plants in all Nature serves so great a purpose. They are Nature's own fertilizer factories that work night and day.

Plants cannot use nitrogen in the pure form. It must be combined with other elements. But it is a stubborn sort of thing that refuses to combine. One way of getting it out of the air is to pass strong currents of electricity through it. There are factories at Niagara where electricity is plentiful, that bring down the nitrogen in this way. The government has spent hundreds of millions of dollars at Muscle Shoals, in Tennessee, in developing electricity for the purpose of taking nitrogen out of the air.

But the bean-bearing plants do it in their roots with the greatest ease. They get nitrogen in the proper form and put it back into the soil. They are the greatest fertilizer factories in the world.

They do it with the help of bacteria. Bacteria are plants that are so small that they can be seen only with a microscope. There are many of them in the soil. Certain kinds of them live on the roots of the bean-bearing plants. Strange to say, they will live on the roots of no other plants. They bore into the roots and set up their homes.

These bacteria in the roots cause swellings or enlargements of them called *galls* or *nodules*. It is in these nodules that these tiny bacteria have their homes. There they set up factories that take the nitrogen out of the air just as do the huge electric plants at Niagara. The sap that circulates through the roots combines in these nodules with the nitrogen of the air and prepares that nitrogen so that it can be used by plants.

In doing this the bacteria and the bean plants work together and both are benefited. The bacteria get the nitrogen which they need and so do the plants. In fact, both get more nitrogen than they need and put what is left over into the soil. In this way the soil is enriched for the benefit of whatever other plants may grow.

All growing plants need nitrogen. They all take it out of the soil. If there is not enough of it there, the plants grow badly or not at all. Sandy tracts, for instance, are likely to have little nitrogen. Few plants will grow

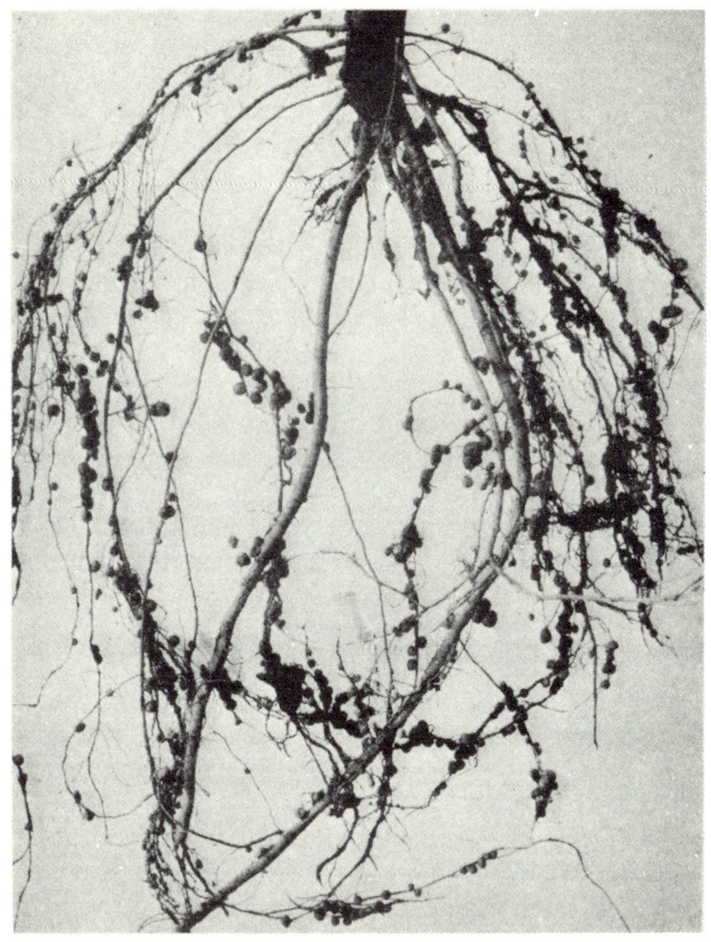

THERE ARE BACTERIA IN THESE NODULES ON THE BEAN ROOTS THAT PUT NITROGEN INTO THE SOIL

on them. Members of the bean family, however, may be planted there and will manufacture their own nitrogen compounds and get along very well. By being grown on sandy land they may build up a supply of nitrogen in the soil that will make it support other plants. Such lands in Florida, for instance, may be built up so that orange groves will thrive on them.

Practically all the plants, except those of the bean group, take nitrogen out of the soil and put none back. If wheat or corn or cotton are grown steadily on a given tract of land, they gradually use up all its nitrogen. Crops grow less and less until it no longer pays to plant them. Such a piece of land is said to be "run down."

The farmers have found that there is a way to "build up" such soils. That way is to plant members of the bean family on them. These plants immediately set their nodule factories to work and begin to put surplus nitrogen into the soil. They also store up much nitrogen in their own bodies. If, after they have got well stocked up with this nitrogen, the farmer will plow them under he will give his soil a double dose of nitrogen.

Only in the last generation have the farmers learned of the possibilities that lie in thus growing a crop of some member of the bean family on their land once in every two or three years. Cowpeas or soy beans or velvet beans are excellent for this purpose and at the same time yield abundant feed for stock.

Year in and year out through the centuries and all around the world the bean-bearing plants have been pouring their richness of nitrogen into the soil. But for the fact that they have done so, this world would be a poor place from the standpoint of the plants it could support. Now that man has learned to hunt out the spots that are poor in nitrogen and deliberately plant beans on them, a huge improvement of soils is taking place. Finding the way to do this has been one of the great discoveries of the age.

There is, in fact, a very complicated world there in the ground at the roots of the bean-bearing plants. It has taken a long time to learn to understand it. There are, for instance, many different kinds of these microscopic bacteria, these plants that are too small to see, just as there are many kinds of trees. One kind of them may be fond of cowpea roots and another kind of clover roots. The cowpea bacteria will have nothing to do with clover roots. It comes to pass that there must be just the right kind of bacteria in the soil to raise one or the other of these crops.

Here is a strange example of what happens when the soil does not have the right sort of bacteria. More than a hundred years ago alfalfa, the most wonderful of the clover-like plants, was brought to the Atlantic seaboard and planted. It grew in a sickly sort of way and finally died out. Much later it got started on the Pacific coast, flourished wonderfully, and slowly worked its way east. Finally the secret of bacteria was discovered. It was found that the right sort of bacteria must be placed in the soil at the same time as the seed. Soil from the West was brought east and scattered with the alfalfa seed, and the crop grew abundantly where before it had languished and died.

So it is with all the members of the bean group. Each must have its own special bacteria in the soil. The bacteria for clover and for beans is now scattered all over the world. Those plants will grow almost anywhere. But when bringing in a new member of the bean family, the scientists know that they must bring along some of the soil in which it has grown, for that soil is sure to have the right bacteria. It must be planted along with the seed.

It would be hard to figure out just how much help these nitrogen-fixing bacteria render to man in raising his crops. Working steadily all over the world all the time as they do, there is little question but that they cause its soil to produce more than it otherwise would. If the result is that it yields ten per cent more crops than it would if it were not getting the nitrogen it needs, the value contributed would be stupendous.

Chapter IV

THE POTATO AND ITS POISONOUS RELATIVES

OF LATE certain family secrets of the plant world, long safely closeted, have been allowed to reveal themselves, and it has come to be understood that one old friend and another among the vegetables is not very well connected. Some of the very best known of them are members of groups that have long been outlawed. They have, however, been so well established in public confidence that now their secrets may be openly discussed without fear of injury.

The potato, for example, is a member of a family of a shockingly bad reputation. It belongs to a group of poison plants. The deadly nightshade, of Old England, gives this family its name. It is the nightshade family. Through the centuries ancestors of Americans, living in England, have cautioned their children against eating the fruit of the nightshade, growing in the fence corners and hedgerows. The plant has berries that are colorful and pretty, as big as cherries, and many an English child has disobeyed and suffered.

In America the Jimson weed belongs to the nightshade family, but offers no attractive fruit to cause trouble. It is poisonous but of such bad odor that there is no temptation to eat its leaves or fruit. When Europeans came to America, they discovered a number of members of the nightshade family, unknown on the other side of the world, which were destined to become famous and have much to do with the affairs of man.

By the form of its leaves and flowers, the tomato is shown to be a nightshade. The white man found it growing wild in America, but became suspicious of it because of its obvious family connections. The fruit,

THE JIMSON WEED IS A USELESS POTATO COUSIN

like that of all nightshades, was admittedly a thing of beauty and, eventually, it was introduced into gardens as an ornamental plant. It was called the *love apple.* It grew there for a hundred years before people began to eat it. When they did begin nibbling it, this love apple was not so good to eat as it is now. The fruits that were the biggest and the best began to be selected for planting, and thus tomatoes were improved in quality. But a hundred years ago they were not much used.

Tomatoes are quite a new food for man. About 1850 the idea of canning them was hit upon and a new industry began to come into being. Today tomatoes are third in rank among the vegetables of this country in volume consumed. A million and a half tons are grown each year.

The eggplant is one of the nightshades that has recently come into use as food. The big red pepper is another. The close kinship between the pepper and the tomato is shown by the recent cross between the two which promises a new salad fruit for man from this poison group.

THE TOBACCO PLANT IS A NIGHTSHADE AND POISONOUS LIKE OTHERS OF THIS FAMILY

Still another of the nightshades, a big brother

of the family, probably as well known as the potato and more far flung in its use, is tobacco. Early voyagers to America found the natives doing a strange thing never known to the Eastern World up to that time. They put fire on what seemed to be the end of a stick and smoked it. On examination it was found that they had rolled up the leaves of one of their native plants, applied light to the end of it, and indulged in the strange practice of drawing the smoke into their mouths.

Sailors learned to smoke, and laid in supplies of tobacco. The natives of many a European seaport town were astonished in the decades that followed to see these sailors about the waterfronts "breathing this fire and smoke." These natives even learned how it was done. Many began to acquire the habit.

The demand for tobacco grew rapidly. Tobacco culture became a great industry in colonial days, especially in Virginia and Maryland, and still survives. This nightshade has become the most widely used plant in the world. Its poison qualities may be tested by anyone who wants to try the experiment of swallowing a quid of it.

When Spaniards went exploring in South America, along the Andes Mountains, they found that the natives were cultivating another American plant of this poison group and were eating what seemed to be a fruit that grew on its underground stems. The natives called this food *papas*—so called to this day. It was their staple food. The same plant grew wild in other parts of America, notably in the Rocky Mountain regions of what is now Colorado, but it did not amount to much. The southern natives had loosened the ground, thus giving the tubers a better chance to grow under the surface. They had covered them from the sun so that they did not acquire that bitterness which they had when exposed to the sun. They had selected the better kinds and bred them. They had well-developed varieties of potatoes, the ancestors of those that have fed the multitudes since that time.

These Spaniards took potatoes back to Europe and there they spread slowly. They became popular first in Italy. Sir Walter Raleigh, after many wanderings in America, also carried potatoes to Europe. He first planted them on his estates near Cork, Ireland, where they became very popular. There was reason for this. The land in Ireland was divided into small tracts and the people needed a crop from which much food could be raised on small tracts of land. The potato met that need. It soon became the food of the Irish people and came to be known as the *Irish potato.* Many people have thought that this American food plant originated in Ireland.

The effect on Ireland was marvelous. The food supply at times had been so short that three millions of people were about all that the island could support. With the potato, however, more people could be nourished than was the case before. The result of its planting was such that, in the 200 years that followed, the population of Ireland increased to eight millions of people. This one poison plant in one small country had brought five million people into being. Since the Irish are one of the sturdiest stocks in the world, and since these teeming numbers came at a time when the waste places of the world were being filled up, it must be admitted that this extra food supply had a considerable effect on the nature of modern man and the making of modern history.

THE POTATO PLANT IS MUCH LIKE ITS NIGHTSHADE COUSINS

But the planting of the potato in Ireland led to a terrible tragedy. By 1840 the country was teeming with its eight million inhabitants. In the ten years that followed there was a blight on the potatoes. There was not enough food to support the people. One million of them died of starvation. Another million saved itself by leaving the country.

In England and France the potato had a hard time getting started. The prejudice against it had much to do with this. A lack of proper care of the potato was another factor. When a part of a growing potato is above the ground, it turns green and bitter. The poison collects at this point. If allowed to lie exposed to the sun, the same thing happens. The potato must grow entirely under the ground and after harvest it should be kept in a dark place. Light brings out its bad qualities.

In France well-informed people knew that potatoes were a good food, but the peasants would have none of them. Louis XIV served them at court and wore a potato bloom in his coat to try to make them popular. A man of science at his court practiced a clever ruse. He planted a field of potatoes and, as they matured, posted a guard about them. The guard, however, was instructed to stop no stealing. The result was that all his crop disappeared, and the peasants began to esteem potatoes and to plant them.

In England Raleigh induced Queen Elizabeth to serve potatoes at the royal banquet. However, they continued to be despised. They were called the *lazy root.* The prejudice against this branch of the nightshade family persisted. A society opposed to eating potatoes was organized. It was called The Society to Prevent Unwholesome Diet. It is said that the word "spud," sometimes applied to the potato, came from the first letters in the words that made up the name of this society. The English are slow in giving up a prejudice or in taking up a new thing. It took hundreds of years to persuade them to eat potatoes.

The potato did not come into its greatest glory until the days of the World War. Then, when many

THE FRUIT OF THE TOMATO PLANT OF THE NIGHTSHADE FAMILY WAS LONG THOUGHT TO BE POISONOUS

nations realized that the outcome of the war depended on the abilities of their peoples to feed themselves, they all turned to this cheap and productive crop.

Especially was this the case in Germany, which was inside the iron ring. The potato crop kept millions alive. After the war was over, the quickest way to obtain a sufficient food crop was by growing the potato. There are many millions alive today who might have died except for the potato.

All members of the nightshade family may be seen to be much alike. There are similarities in their structure, in their flowers, in their fruit, that mark them as close kinsmen. They are more nearly alike than the members of most of the plant families. It is easier to see that they are kin than it is to see that the apple belongs to the rose family, that the onion is a lily, or that the locust tree is a cousin to the modest bean bush in the garden. All of these relationships will be recognized, however, if one will only begin to look for family traits among plants.

The fact that the potato plant grows its tubers underground is one of the unusual devices to which plants resort that they may be sure that there will be others of their kind coming into the world each year. Plants take great care of their seeds. Most of them are satisfied to have the seeds grow on their tops from blossoms. A few go out of their way to make doubly sure of their seeds. The potato is one of these. It produces a flower which develops a seed from which a new generation of plants may grow. But to make doubly sure the potato grows a tuber in the ground also. A new plant may come from it in the spring. Thus it employs two methods of carrying on its race.

Each potato has several "eyes." From each of these, if the circumstances are right, a plant will grow when spring comes. A potato grower may either plant the seed or he may cut up the potatoes themselves and plant the "eyes." The latter method gets quicker results.

Because the potato plant has taken this unusual precaution to make sure of its children, man was given this crop which, though a comparatively new one, has proved to be one of the most important in the world. There are more tons of potatoes produced in the world than of any other crop. It furnishes one-fourth of the food of the people of Europe who accepted it so reluctantly. Its use is steadily increasing. Scientists continually are improving its quality. They are showing farmers how to grow more of it to the acre. Its importance seems destined to increase as the world becomes more densely populated.

Many things in the nature of the potato show that its use as a food will increase. In the first place, the yield to the acre is exceedingly high. In Europe, where people are careful about their cultivation, the average potato yield is 10,000 pounds to the acre. The same acre will yield only 1,000 pounds of wheat. In the second place, the potato will yield these abundant crops in a very short season. It requires only about a hundred days in which to grow a crop. Summers are short in most of Europe. They are short in northern United States. The northern part of Maine is an ideal potato section. Summer days are long and hot. The growing season is, however, so short that it would be impossible to mature a crop such as corn. Consequently the potato becomes an especial blessing to the northern states, because its native home was in the high mountains, in the Andes and in the Rockies, where the seasons are short. Then the potato, like its nightshade cousin, the tomato, is not over particular about soil. These twins will produce food on almost any patch of land.

The potato is an inconceivably better article of food now than it was when the Spaniards found it in Peru. The scientists' lore of plant breeding and selection has been applied to it with marvelous results. In principle here is the way it has worked:

A potato grower finds that certain plants in his field are better than the others. By keeping the seeds or tubers from these for planting he gets better potatoes. He then selects the prize plants in this second generation and fertilizes the flowers of one of these with the pollen of another. He selects the best plants in the next generation and uses these for seed. Thus the quality of his potatoes steadily is improved.

It has been found that a potato with a smooth surface saves much work in peeling. One breeder may develop such a potato. Perhaps, however, the plant that grows such a potato is not a heavy producer. Part of its potatoes are undersize. This model potato must be crossed with one whose tubers all grow to full size. This is another ten-year task in breeding. The potatoes that result may prove to be subject to disease. A blight may attack them. It may be found, however, that a few plants are not affected. They have some peculiar quality of resistance to the disease. The breeder will examine these plants carefully. He may find one that has potatoes of the right degree of smoothness, that develops its potatoes to a uniform and proper size, that has not been affected by the blight. He will grow new potatoes from this plant. He may establish a variety that may become famous around the world. Many men have done just such things as this. They have contributed to the food supply of the world in quantities that are impossible to measure. They have led this plant of bad family to increased usefulness.

Through the ages man has come in contact with the things about him and has learned to make use of one and another of them. He found a jungle hen in India, the only bird in the world with wattles, developed it into the chicken of the barnyard and carried it all around the world. He found a wild bee that stored honey in a hollow tree, studied its habits, built better homes for it, coaxed it to gather more honey than it needed for its own family, and took his toll. He took a fluttering little moth, studied its habits, found that its young, at a certain stage of their lives, spun a floss for which he might find a use. He made domestic animals of this moth and its young ones, developed silkworm farming, and built up an industry that is one of the marvels of the world. But none of these accomplishments is greater than the use he has made of the poisonous nightshades.

Chapter V

THE VILLAINOUS DAISY

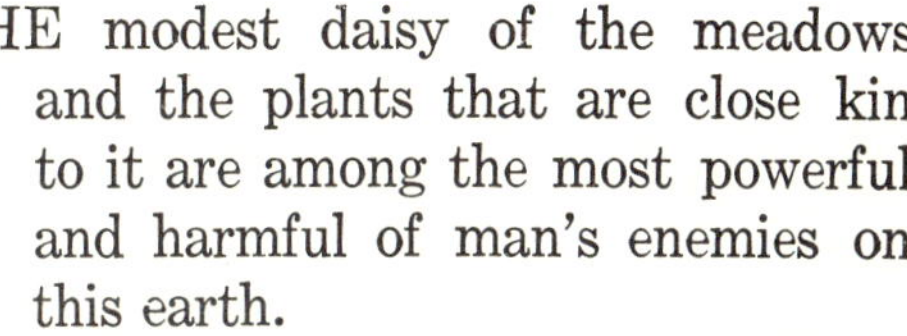

THE modest daisy of the meadows and the plants that are close kin to it are among the most powerful and harmful of man's enemies on this earth.

One is not likely to think of a black-eyed Susan, or the modest bachelor's-button, or the shining dandelion, or the aster in the corner of the garden, or the goldenrod growing by the roadside, or the flaming devil's paint brush, as enemies of mankind. They grow very humbly in the open field or the fence corner and look out mildly at the passer-by.

One may realize easily that the hardy sunflower, the dusty ragweed, the common bull thistle, may crowd in upon man's preserves and give him trouble. They are vigorous plants and may be expected to use their elbows.

As a matter of fact, all these are members of the daisy family. It is sometimes called the *sunflower family* and by the botanists the *composite family*. They are herbs, plants whose tops die down every year, as distinguished from shrubs which keep alive above ground. All the members of the daisy family are generally classified as weeds. Weeds are plants that insist on growing where they are unwelcome, in places which man has set aside for his own crops. They interfere with those crops.

They therefore lose their popularity with those who grow crops. They are set down by the farmer as enemies.

Modest as most members of the daisy family seem to be, they have the advantage of numbers. Of all the families of flowering plants, the daisy family is the largest. There are more brothers and sisters, aunts and uncles, first, second, and third cousins in the daisy family than in any other.

The flowers of the daisy group are easy to recognize. They are fundamentally different from the flowers of any other plants. They are called *composite flowers* by botanists because each flower is made up of many small florets.

An examination of a daisy or, better still, of a sunflower will show that scores of blooms are bound together in a single ring. Those on the outside do the advertising for the group by sending out petals to attract the insects that bring pollen to them. Many of the most beautiful of the cultivated flowers of the garden are members of this family and may be recognized by their composite blooms.

The head of a ripe sunflower after the seeds are formed shows the floret grouping very well. Every seed comes from one of the florets in the group. Yet it is the group and not the individuals that make it up that is thought of as the flower of this plant.

There are practical advantages to the plant family in clubbing together in this way. When the honeybee, with pollen on its hairy head, visits a flower of the daisy group, it is likely to make a sort of pot shot, to shake

THE COMPOSITE FLOWER, WITH A CIRCLE OF SEEDS IN THE CENTER, IS VERY EFFICIENT

some of that pollen into a score of the individual blooms, thus fertilizing the larger number.

The common white daisy of the field beautifies the early summer, furnishes children with an abundance of flowers from which to weave daisy chains and tells maidens whether "he loves me" or "he loves me not," but it was not to be found in all America when settlers from Europe first came. These settlers brought it with them from the old country.

Very often ships coming to American shores for cargoes were not heavily loaded as they sailed west and they carried earth and other waste as ballast to make them ride the waves properly. Before loading in America, they dumped this ballast. Often it contained seeds of many sorts, some of them weeds that started growing and caused the American farmer endless trouble.

Ballast dumping has sowed weed seed from Europe all around the coasts of the United States. They also came hidden away in the seed of clover or wheat that was sent across for planting in the new land. It was in some such way that the daisy came. But, having arrived, it found endless stretches of open country in which it might bloom undisturbed. So the daisy population of America increased without end.

Daisies yield no crops of value to man. His cattle refuse to eat daisies. Yet the daisies crowd out the clovers and the useful grasses. They take up much valuable space in the fields. They drink up the moisture and eat the plant food that might otherwise go into crop plants. They reduce the productiveness of the farms.

The modest dandelion, cousin to the daisy, hugs the earth and thrives all over the world. "Dent de lion" the name was at first, meaning "lion's tooth." There is doubt whether there exists in all America a single lawn on which these squat plants are not to be found with their leaves making a sturdy rosette that crowds out the grass. Although the lawn mower may cut off their tops every week in the year, their stubborn roots persist and sooner or later the plant is likely to find a chance to burst into that golden yellow bloom which, it must be admitted, has its points of beauty.

There is no more efficient seed maker in all the world than the dandelion. Every one of the scores of small blooms that go to make up its composite flower has a honey cup that invites members of the insect world. Most of the insects that visit flowers come to see the dandelion. These many and frequent visits give ample assurance that every compartment of the flowers will be fertilized. The result is that this flower yields scores of seeds to guarantee the crop of the next year.

THE DANDELION BALL HOLDS A THOUSAND SEEDS READY TO RIDE AWAY ON THE WIND

Of all plants, none has a surer method of scattering its seeds broadcast than the dandelion. Every child is familiar with the airy, fluffy ball in which the dandelion packs its seeds. What child has not held one of these in his hand, blown upon it, and watched it dissolve into a thousand particles that floated away on the wind? Each of these particles carried a dandelion seed. Each seed was provided with a parachute so made as to catch and ride the winds. No dependence on chance or the favor of some member of the animal kingdom in its seed planting. It rides the winds all over the world.

And wherever it goes, it is likely to fight for its plot of earth which man may be wanting to use for other crops. So do the humble and the great come into conflict.

Quite unlike the earth-loving dandelion is its haughty cousin, the towering sunflower. The wild sunflower loves the grain fields of America. It is native to the Western Hemisphere but had never been seen by white man before Columbus. Its bloom, radiating petals, might have been an artist's picture of the sun. It is a popular belief that the face of this flower daily follows the sun from east to west, but this is not a fact.

This sunflower may grow to a considerable height. It may quite overrun a cultivated field. It is one of the rankest of weeds. Pioneers have fought it in their clearings ever since they began to settle in the West. By cutting the stalk as it approaches seed-making time, one may leave it with no seed for next year's crop. Infinitely hard labor through the decades has gone into this destruction of sunflowers.

Some philosopher has said that a weed is a plant for which no use has been found. The sunflower came near saving itself from the weed classification, for there is a variety of it that is grown as a farm product. Three hundred years ago Europeans, penetrating to the shores of Lake Huron, found the Indians cultivating a variety of this hardy American flower. These Indians must have known the law of selective plant breeding. Beginning with the wild sunflower, they had, through the years, selected the larger specimens for seed. Their flowers grew larger and larger, until they were sometimes half a foot across. Their seeds were large and grainlike.

They made excellent food for man and beast. Europeans took them back across the Atlantic and they became widely grown in door yards. They became better known in Europe than in America. For a long time there was mystery as to the origin of this domestic sunflower, widely grown in Europe and less familiar in America which was the native home of its wild brother. Finally

DANDELIONS

the plant was traced back to New York's Indians who were interested in agriculture.

The development of this huge sunflower calls to mind the parallel case of the chrysanthemum evolved, through patient selection by the Chinese, from bigger and better daisies as parents for the new generations.

It is estimated that these daisy cousins, these composite-flowered plants, make up nine per cent of all the flowering plants. They are, of course, very important in the plant world. Because of their numbers, it is unfortunate that so many of them are actually harmful to man. It would not do to say that they serve no purpose, for at least they do lend limitless beauty to the great out-of-doors.

THE GOLDENROD LENDS GLORY TO THE AUTUMN

The goldenrod, for example, adorns the countryside during the autumn months with the warmth of its colorful flowers. The brilliant yellow of it is the dominant color of the members of the family. There are flowers of other colors, such as the red of the devil's paint brush, the purple of the New England aster, and the blue of the chickory. But yellow is the dominant color of these composites. The goldenrod, with the flower efficiency of its kind, offers the favorite autumn food supply for the honey-eating insects. It has throngs of visitors always about its door. The under side of these visitors are always smeared with pollen from other flowers which they have visited. By merely crawling across a flower's face, these insects may fertilize scores of the tiny florets, each of which, as a result, brings forth seed for a new generation.

The goldenrod loves the edges of woods and glens. It blossoms into an autumn "cloth of gold" in abandoned fields where deserted cabins stand as monuments to the restlessness of the race from which we came; it paints the hillsides where rocky bluffs look down on rugged oak trees; and it warms October days in all the byways of the countryside.

Then, finally, there is the thistle, most troublesome of all the members of the daisy family, which, from Biblical times, has typified the obnoxious weed of waste places. It is not without beauty, to be sure, when its rose-purple brush is often given to bloom with the painted lady butterfly, whose eggs are laid on this plant, hovering above it.

The thistle is a forbidding plant. From tip to root it is studded with bristles that repel all invaders. Few of the browsing animals will put mouth to the thistle; few will eat hay with which thistles are mixed. Even the ant, which climbs many honey-producing plants to steal from the store prepared for the bees, can scarcely reach the thistle blossom. So many are the spines put in his way that he is constantly pushed out from the stalk for a fall. Thus it comes to pass that, by repelling all enemies, the thistle blossom usually succeeds in blooming and in bearing seeds.

The thistle shows its relationship to the modest dandelion. Its seed pod is a downy globe where every member is provided with a parachute, ready to take to the air. Thistledown has come to typify the lightest of substances given to traveling down the wind. Thus are its legions broadcast into wider fields.

The worst one of them is the Canada thistle. It really is a European thistle which was recognized as a curse before America was discovered. It is not unlike other thistles above ground, but underneath it has peculiarities of root that make it the most difficult to fight.

Most thistles start with a sturdy root, like the dandelion, and a rosette of leaves hugging the ground. Often they attempt to produce no flower or seed the first year of their growth. The root lives through the winter and the second season the top grows high, blooms, and sends out its thistledown. The thistle is usually a biennial or two-year plant.

The Canada thistle, however, has a way of its own of living forever and of spreading, although it makes no seed. Beneath the ground it sends out roots in every direction. These roots may reach out several feet from its base. Then from the joints of the roots new plants grow. Thus one plant multiplies into a multitude. Chop it down, prevent it from making seed, and it will keep alive underground. It becomes so thick in a field that it crowds out all other vegetation. Plow the land and the roots merely turn over and send up new shoots. There are few pests in this world that are harder to deal with than the Canada thistle.

Laws have been passed against this thistle. Dealers have been forbidden to sell seed that has the slightest sprinkling of the thistle seed. Farmers have been forbidden to allow it to go to seed on their land. The government has issued bulletins setting out the ways in which it can be destroyed, once it begins to dispute the ownership of a piece of land. A glance at a thistle campaign might give an idea of some of the difficulties of these fights against this weed.

The botanist knows that it is in the leaves that the food of plants is prepared. The leaves of the Canada thistle, with the aid of the water brought up from underground, have taken much food from the air and stored it up in these stubborn roots. They can live for a long time on their stored food, but not forever. If they can be prevented from getting food, they will in the end be starved to death.

The botanist found that, by keeping the thistle roots from making any leaves above ground, the Canada thistle could not survive. Consequently, some crop that calls for a good deal of cultivation, such as corn, is planted, so that it may be cultivated both ways. This cultivation will destroy every thistle leaf that appears. The farmer must go over the ground with a hoe to cut the thistles that appear too close to the cornstalk to be reached by the cultivator. He may starve the thistles in a single year. It requires careful work, but this is about the only way to get results.

Some people believe that this great family of composite plants, most of them weeds, are gaining on man and that the time will come when they will overrun the world. Certain it is that they are among man's worst enemies.

There are many other plants that are classed as weeds. Many members of the grass family are weeds. Grasses call for more cultivation of crops, for more use of the plow and the hoe, than does the daisy family. Tumbleweeds, cockleburs, beautiful poppies of the wheat fields, wild clover, mustard, Jimson weed, all are troublesome weeds. Altogether the government figures that these weeds cost the farmer of the United States a hundred million dollars a year by their crowding in on crops and robbing them of the plant food and moisture that is in the soil. But, the philosopher responds, man's plant friends are without number. Directly or indirectly, they feed him from the cradle to the grave. Under the circumstances he should be willing to entertain an occasional unwilling guest.

Chapter VI

WHEAT, OF THE GRASS FAMILY

ONE MAY not think of wheat as a grass, but it is. It is even less likely that one should think of sugar cane or of sorghum as grasses. And field corn is just as much a grass as is the covering of the trim lawn which one sprinkles on summer evenings. And the giant bamboo of Japan and China, known to have grown to a height of one hundred fifty feet and used in house building, is a grass.

Some of these grasses are giants and some are Lilliputians. They are, however, all built on the same plan. The grass leaf is not like that of other plants. One usually speaks of a "blade" of grass. Grasses generally have tassels at the top which bear their seeds in a different way from the familiar flowering plants. But, most striking of all, they are jointed plants. They build up their stalks differently from other plants.

THE MEMBERS OF THE GRASS FAMILY HAVE LEAVES THAT ARE CALLED BLADES BECAUSE OF THEIR SHAPE

Most grasses produce one section after another of hollow tubing. A wheat straw is a perfect example of this. In corn the tube is filled with pith. Ask any construction engineer and he will tell you that if he takes a pound of any building material such as steel, he can get more strength out of it if made into a hollow tube than in any other form. Grasses build their stalks on the hollow tube scheme, tied together here and there by joints. Thus they get strength with lightness. This hollow tube is their own invention. Plants are always members of the grass family if they are found to have these joints and bladelike leaves.

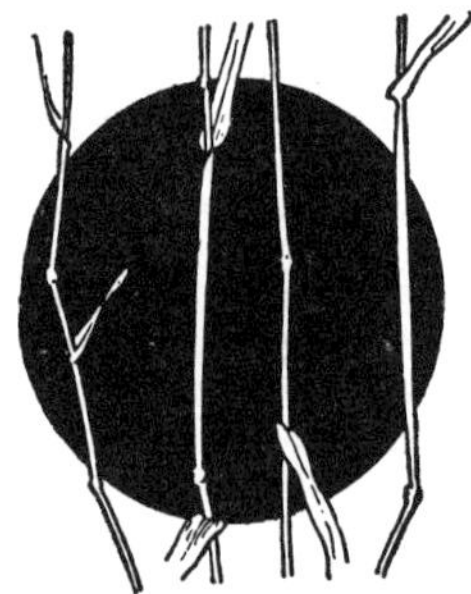

GRASS STEMS ARE BUILT UP JOINT BY JOINT

Grasses are not usually thought of as having flowers, but, as a matter of fact, they flower just as do lilies or daisies. Their tassels at first are clusters of flowers. They seldom use bright colors or emit odors, however, as do many of the flowering plants. They do not have honey in their cups as do other flowers. Flowering plants do these things to attract the bees that bring them pollen. The grasses do not need the help of the bees. They make their own pollen in such a form that the wind, wafting it about, will fertilize them.

The grass family is one of the most important to man in all the vegetable kingdom. There is no question but that it does more toward feeding man than any other. Possibly it does more than all the others together.

One has only to recall a few of the useful grasses to realize their importance. Wheat, for example, is the most important bread-making grain in the world, and bread to the Western World is the staff of life. Rice is a grass that is a first cousin of wheat. It feeds the countless multitudes of the Orient, whose fight for food is so intense and never ends. It probably feeds more people than does wheat, but from the Western viewpoint it is not nearly so important.

WHEAT GROWING IN A FIELD

Corn, which is the biggest crop of the United States, year by year sells for more money than any other. Various sorghums feed millions in Africa and parts of Asia, especially India and China. The sugar of the world is largely made from a grass, sugar cane. Oats, rye, and barley are grasses. The pasturage of the world which feeds man's live stock, furnishing him meat and dairy products, is chiefly grass. It covers the earth, beautifies it, keeps the rain from cutting it to pieces. Grass, in fact, is man's main dependence. Were it not for the plant family with the plan of tying itself together by joints, man might have a hard time getting on in the world.

Wheat has been a humble servitor of man for a very long time. When students of early man dig into the ruins of dead civilizations, they are very sure to find the charred remains of wheat. The Lake Dwellers of Switzerland left such remains. So did the Egyptians in their tombs and pyramids. So also did the Israelites in Canaan. In all these cases the wheat remains that have been found are of well-developed grains. This shows us that the crop had been grown by civilizations that had preceded the early Egyptians. Wheat was a food of the races from which Western civilization sprang.

It is reasonable to suppose that wheat, in the beginning, was a wild grass which grew seeds that wild man began to gather and eat. Finally, this wild man learned to plant this grass around his dwelling place. Naturally he selected for planting the grass that gave him the best seeds. This selection, which has been the fundamental principle of plant improvement through the centuries, steadily built up a grass that gave a more and more satisfactory seed food for man.

Thus the civilizations of Greece and Rome found that much had been done for them through the centuries that had gone before. Wheat spread with the growth of civilization. With it developed methods of grinding that increased the usefulness of the crop. The black bread of the Middle Ages was a crude product of wheat due to the impurities that got into the flour in the grinding. For centuries wheat was made into flour by pounding it between two stones. Then two heavy stones were fitted to roll on each other and the flour mill was evolved. The windmill and the water wheel came into being, with them the miller ground flour for the community. Finally the modern flour mill was built to grind thousands of barrels of flour for shipment all over the world. Recently huge bakeries have been developed to make flour into bread for the multitude. Thus man's chief food, a product of grass, comes to him ready to eat.

Wheat came to what is now the United States with the early settlers, getting a start with the Virginia colony as early as 1618 and in New England somewhat later. It moved westward with the advance of settlement. The fifty years between 1790 and 1840 was the canal-building era. These artificial waterways furnished a means of transportation that had not existed before. They aided the settlement of western New York, the Lake region, and the Ohio Valley.

At this time the implements of production and harvesting were crude and were not adapted to growing wheat on a large scale. Much of the seeding was still done by hand. The sickle and the cradle were used for harvesting and the flail for threshing, the only power back of them being the strong arms of the farmers. The reaper was then in progress of development and first came into use in 1826. It was still a long way to the heading machine and the thresher and finally to the combined harvester-thresher.

The stupendous strides in wheat production in the United States is shown by the fact that in another fifty years, between 1870 and 1920, the crop had multiplied threefold. By 1920 there were 2,000,000 farmers in the

United States who were growing wheat. A half acre of wheat was harvested each year for each man, woman, and child in the country. The great mass of the population ate wheat products in one form or another three times a day. It furnished the most important elements in the food of the nation.

The seed of this wild grass that man had tamed in the dawn era of his development, in fact, became important

GRAIN COMBINES MOVING THROUGH WHEAT FIELD

to most of the nations of the world and its distribution at times a matter of life and death. The wheat growers of the United States have a vital interest in the wheat production of other countries, because the price of wheat on the farms in the United States is determined in large measure by the prices paid in the world markets. Certain countries stand out as large producers of wheat. European countries produce large quantities of wheat, but most of them consume large quantities also. The important surplus-producing countries which compete with the United States in the world markets are Canada, India, Russia, Argentina, and Australia.

Wheat is not grown to any extent in the warm, humid sections of the world. It is confined almost entirely to regions with temperate climates. Where the moisture is not excessive, it may be grown in relatively warm climates, as in northern Africa, India, and Mexico. To the North, in Canada and Russia, production is limited by too short growing seasons. In Australia and Argentina, as well as in some parts of North America and Asia, expansion of area is limited by lack of precipitation. There are no available statistics of wheat production in China. Some wheat is grown in China, but the great food crops of the people in that part of the world are rice, various millets, and sorghums. Within the area suitable for growing wheat, it must compete with other grain crops such as oats, corn, barley, and rye.

The large number of producers tends to stabilize the markets and, under normal conditions, to insure the world's bread supply. The crops of Russia and the United States constitute a large part of the world crop, but frequently when the crops of the United States are good, the Russian crop is short. Thus the several countries supplement each other in producing wheat for the world markets.

There have been many strange and romantic problems in this development of the stupendous wheat crop of the United States. Some have had to do with the efforts of science to improve the crop. Some have had to do with the battles that have been fought to protect it from its enemies. One of the worst of these has been that with black-stem rust which sometimes gets into the wheat fields and ruins the crop. It is a strange story, how the black-stem rust comes about.

It all ties back, for instance, to the barberry bush, which has for hundreds of years had its place as an ornamental shrub in the yards of Europeans and Americans. This bush was brought to America by the settlers and has been carried west by them. It has escaped their gardens and run wild in the woods. It makes possible black-stem rust, which cannot exist without it.

This rust is a plant, so small that its spores or "seeds" may be seen only with the microscope. It lives through the winter on the straw of the field. When spring comes, its spores, blown by the wind, find their way to the barberry bushes. There the rust develops and prospers until the wheat fields are well developed. Then the rust makes another pilgrimage. It again rides away on the wind and finds new homes in the wheat.

In the northern states the winter spores develop rust in the spring only on barberry bushes. In the very midst of the World War, for example, the rust from barberry bushes got into the wheat in Minnesota and caused the loss of 200,000,000 bushels of it just at the time when the very outcome of the war might have depended on feeding troops with this same wheat. Where there are no barberry bushes in the North, there will be no rust when the wheat comes. If the barberry bushes could be destroyed, there would be no more epidemics of black-stem rust. The government is trying to kill all the barberry bushes. It has not yet succeeded in doing so. In the meantime the damage goes on.

Black-stem rust ties into another situation that smacks of romance. In the year 1877, there was a boy by the name of Mark Carleton who lived on a farm in Cloud County, Kansas, strangely so named because those sprinkling pots of the air were so seldom seen there. Cloud County is in the dry section of Kansas.

Ten years later, Mark Carleton was given a degree by a frontier college, having specialized in botany. He taught botany for a while, but often fled from the schoolroom to the open fields. He worked for years at the Kansas Experiment Station trying to find a solution to the riddle of the rust. The result was failure. He went to Washington with another idea. Just as there are some people who do not take the mumps, possibly there is wheat somewhere in the world that does not suffer from black rust. Would the government allow him to try to find such a wheat? It would. He sent to the different states and to all parts of the world, asking for sample packages of choice wheats. He sowed a thousand plots on a farm near Washington, each plot to a wheat from a different corner of the world. Most of these wheats grew and prospered in this mild climate. Then he took them

ARISTOCRATS AMONG WHEAT VARIETIES

to the very trying climate of Kansas, planted them, and met in succession two very severe winters. Many of his wheats were winter-killed, especially at Manhattan, Kansas, in 1896–97. Rust attacked his wheats. He got no important results. Thousands of settlers in Kansas who were attempting to grow wheat had failed. They were leaving their prairie farms and going back whence they had come.

But Carleton still tramped the prairies and studied wheat. It was then that he made a discovery. He found a settlement of Russians that were sticking to Kansas. Their crops had not failed. He wondered why. He studied the wheat that they had grown. It was a hard red winter wheat that had begun to get hold in Kansas. It was called *turkey wheat,* the Russians told him. But it was not from Turkey. They had brought it with them when they came from Taurida, Russia. Kansas winters were mild compared with those of Taurida. It was a hard wheat. That was the trouble. The soft wheat mills could not grind it. That was thirty years ago. Now the hard wheats are at a premium. All the choice flours are made from them.

Carleton studied Russia. He found that it had the same black soil as the Great Plains. It was as bleak, as windy, as dry. Yet wheats had been grown on these plains for hundreds of years. His training as a botanist told him that during all that time the weakling wheats had been killed, that only the hardy specimens had lived to become seed for crops that could endure these hard conditions. The wheats of the American Northwest had had no such schooling for their tasks. They were not especially fitted to the region. They had merely been planted there by accident. There had been a selection of the fittest to survive under hard conditions in Russia through the centuries. There must be hardy wheats in Russia, better even than those brought by these chance immigrants, that would whip winter cold and summer drought on the Great Plains. He would find those wheats.

There followed nights of struggle with the Russian language, days of eloquence in arguing official Washington into sending him to the Russian steppes. In the end he won. This hulking, stoop-shouldered, slouch-hatted American traveled over much of Russia. He asked Russians, high and low, about their cold-resistant, their drought-resistant wheats. He took samples of those that were recommended. He pushed on across the endless Russian plains. He crossed the Urals into Siberia. It grew colder, windier, drier. The black earth was a powder in his hand. This was the end of the road. There was nothing worse than this to conquer on the Great Plains.

Here was a wheat, a spring wheat, strong, vigorous, amber-grained, defiant under these trying conditions. Its heads were flat. They were so covered with beards that they looked like barley to this American. He got samples of this wheat from yellow, slant-eyed natives, cousins to the Chinese, who lived in skin-covered huts on the endless steppes. The wheat was of the durum group, which he knew, and hoped had certain superior qualities. It was shipped home as Kubanka durum. It was destined to redeem 4,000,000 acres of the Northwest, too cold and

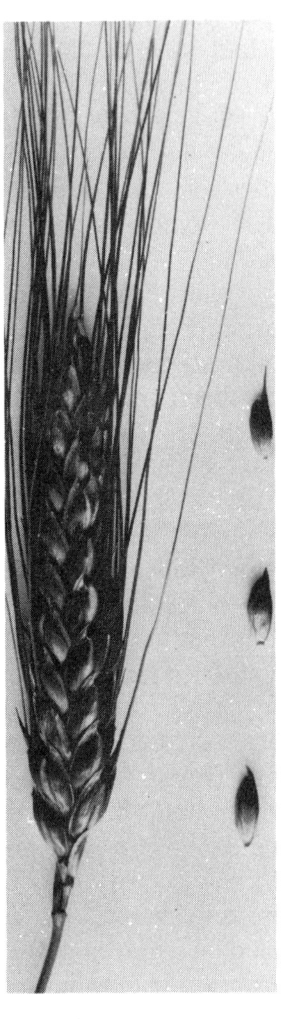

SOME WHEATS HAVE LONG BEARDS

too dry for other wheats, and to add $50,000,000 a year to the nation's pocketbook down through the decades.

Mr. Carleton went back to Russia in 1900, in connection with his work on the Jury of Awards for cereals at the Paris Exposition of that year, primarily to get hard red winter wheats more resistant to cold. He was fully familiar with them, as we learned, and knew that they were increasing rapidly in acreage in that section of the country. The strains that he brought back, such as Kharkof, Beloglina, and others, have helped greatly in furnishing material for breeding and selection to extend the culture of these wheats to the northward.

Carleton himself carried his durum to the experiment stations in the dry country all the way from the Panhandle of Texas to the Canadian border. He had it planted and it yielded abundantly and surely except in the South. Farmers took to it everywhere. It promised to save their dry land farms for them. But it was hard and the mills could not grind it. Carleton fought for the erection of mills that would. Durum won slowly with Nature on its side. Then came the fateful year of 1904, which was to carry the glow of success to the heart of Carleton in a way that he least expected.

That year the black-stem rust struck the Great Plains. Everywhere wheat fields were blanched. Yet not quite everywhere, it seemed, for there were here and there reports of normal yields. These yields were of the new wheat, the durum that had come out of Russia. It was standing up where other crops failed. It was not a victim of the black-stem rust. The dream of Carleton had come true without his expecting it, for the favorite of all his wheat introductions could successfully defy that ancient enemy of the wheat lands.

The fight for better wheat goes on through the decades and through the generations. The federal government leads in it but the states contribute much. Between them they give good demonstrations of one of the practical contributions of government to the well-being of the people.

Chapter VII

CORN AND ITS CULTIVATION

EACH summer day the cornstalks of the United States draw $16,000,000 from the fertile soil. By the end of a span of 120 days that lies between June 1 and October 1 of each year, $2,000,000,000 of new wealth has been thus created. In September the golden harvest of that greatest of crops is near at hand. It equals in value a combination of its three nearest competitors, cotton, hay, and wheat. A little later the task of this titan of the soil is completed for the year and its great contribution to man's comfort has been made.

Corn is another gift of the great grass family of plants, for corn is a grass, as is shown by its jointed body and bladelike leaves. It is another contribution of America to the world, for corn was not known to Europeans before they found it cultivated by the Indians of the Western Hemisphere. The East developed wheat, the West gave corn, each helping along toward feeding man and beast. As the grass from which wheat came is lost in the Old World, so is that which was the ancestor of corn in the New World. Corn, like wheat, has been so long grown under man's care that it will no longer live in the wild state. There are wild grasses that are somewhat like it, as, for example, the fodder grasses of

Mexico, that may be the varieties from which corn came, but whether they are or not, nobody knows.

The gold of the Incas and the Aztecs was a mere trifle in value when compared with the germ of the corn crops of the future that were handed down by the Indians that Columbus discovered. The yellow metal that is being laboriously extracted from the mines of the world is unimportant when compared with the yellow corn which the roots, that claim America for their own, are annually taking from the fertile earth in the broad reaches of her farms. Corn produces a wealth each year that, measured in dollars, makes an amount so great that the mind is incapable of grasping it. Five great freight trains, such as haul the coal from the mines of Pennsylvania, would need to be laden with pure gold to make up the value of the nation's corn crop for a single year.

A realization of these stupendous facts have been bearing down for the last few years upon the men of affairs in the nation who take thought of its welfare. From the government corn has gained part of the recognition to which it is entitled. Wise men who weigh national prosperity in the balance and seek so to adjust the scales as to keep the beam on the rise, have come to think much of corn. They have studied the requirements of this greatest of wealth producers. They have inquired into the conditions under which it does its work. They have taken thought of improving those conditions. They have met problems. They have worked out solutions. They have found methods of benefiting corn in return for the good that corn has done them. They are ready to announce their findings.

EARS OF CORN

It might be well to go along a bit with these men who study methods of improving the plants that feed us, to see how they work and what results they get. Here, for example, is what they say about corn:

"If the farmers of the nation not now practicing seed-corn selection, will resort to the simple device of choosing for planting only the ears of corn from the most productive plants in their fields, their acre yield will increase beyond belief. Heavy corn yields year after year can be maintained only by continuing this seed selection.

"Increased acreage yields of corn repeatedly have been obtained through testing the germination of the seed corn before planting. Under occasional conditions twenty per cent of the seeds planted fail to grow. Yet presence of the life germ in this seed may be tested easily before planting.

"The average corn production of the country is twenty-six bushels to the acre. Yet there are many men in all sections who are producing twice that amount, some who are producing three times as much, and a few who are producing four times as much. Most farmers could increase their yields toward these higher figures by timely attention to the details of successful corn growing."

There are advantages to be derived from a more intelligent cultivation of the crop, through a right preparation of the soil, through proper fertilization, through a revitalizing rotation of crops, through drainage, through right harvesting. There are many things with reference to corn growing that call for the necessity of taking thought. Since corn growing is the life business of many farmers, there would seem to be no reason why thought should not be given to it. This taking thought on the part of the farmer might easily result in raising the present amount of corn more economically on a smaller acreage, thus providing better profits and allowing the farmer to use the additional acreage for other purposes. At any rate, a study of America's prime crop has resulted in the compilation of information that would be worth much each year to the American farmer if he saw fit to use it. It is now up to the farmer.

The consolidated rural schools are teaching the farm boys the principles of growing corn. All over the country many thousands of youngsters are banded together in boys' corn clubs and raising, in competition with each other, an acre of corn under scientific direction. Evidence of what proper methods may accomplish is provided by their acre yields. Their average crops on land on which their fathers were growing fifteen bushels to the acre range from fifty to one hundred bushels. The coming generation is being shown how to multiply the nation's greatest crop and will soon be applying that knowledge. Corn growing is being made the basis of agricultural education.

After a survey of the field, the students of the situation decided that the first step toward the improvement should be in the use of improved seed. They found that some farmers, when planting time came, used for seed the corn that was left over in the crib.

The first step toward improvement was to go to this crib and select from the stock found there only the best ears of corn. These selected ears were planted side by side with the unselected seed. The result of the first crop harvested was a yield of five bushels to the acre more from the selected seed than from the common stock. So far the taking thought had paid magnificently and the added profit had come from the same amount of cultivation as of old.

At first it was thought that this crib selection was all that was necessary. But in the corn so produced, it was noted that while the ears were generally of a good grade the stalks were often inferior. Another method was that of selecting the seed corn while it still stood in the field and of considering not only the ear but the stalk upon which it stood. In this way not only a better ear was reproduced but a better stalk also. An additional two bushels to the acre can be produced by this sort of selection.

New possibilities developed as more attention was paid to seed corn. It was found that in corn, as in other things, the strong parent did not always breed strong offspring. There was a sufficient number of ears that failed to breed true to bring down the general average of the crop. An effort was begun to test each individual ear.

When a number of prize ears had been selected from prize stalks, half the corn from each ear was planted in a given row and the balance was retained. In this way, a record was made of many ears of corn represented in many rows. When harvest time came, the test was applied to the corn of given ears. Those that had bred true were approved and those that failed to produce well were discarded. The remaining portions of the proved ears were used in an isolated patch where only seed corn was grown.

CORNSTALKS

In the course of these experiments many things were discovered incidentally. For instance, it was found that the vitality of corn not thoroughly dried might be greatly reduced by freezing or heating. If seed corn was exposed to freezing before thoroughly dry, or stored where it would heat or mold, its vitality was reduced. The same kind of corn that had been dried quickly produced a stronger plant and yielded more corn to the acre in the coming year. In this way the advisability of drying and storing seed corn separately and caring for it was proved. Special racks in which each ear might be stored and kept in the ideal condition were devised and another step was made toward ideal seed.

It sometimes pays mightily to test each individual ear of seed corn to prove whether or not it germinates properly. The test for germination should be made six weeks before planting time. The ears to be tested should be numbered for identification. Several folds of Canton flannel should be placed in the bottom of a shallow box and the top one of these should be checked into squares and also numbered. Then half a dozen grains should be taken from different portions of a given ear and placed on the square of the same number. The cloth in the bottom of the box is moistened. After the seeds are placed, the box is covered with another damp cloth, then with a piece of glass or oilcloth. If all the representative seeds from a given ear sprout vigorously, the ear is fit for seed. If any fail, it should be discarded.

At about this phase of the investigation, the romance of the corn, the manner in which the tassel woos the silk, began to come in for scientific study and application.

The botanists, of course, know of the relationship of the silk, that the ear of corn grows as it reaches the prime of its young vigor, to the tassel that waves at the top of the plant.

The tassel produces the pollen. That pollen must reach the silk of the ear to fertilize it. The principle of a transfer of pollen that holds in the common flowers applies here but the method is a little different. The tassel depends on the winds to carry its pollen. Through the still summer days it sifts down through the stalks. The silk of the corn drinks in the particles of the pollen that the wind brings and bears them to the grains of corn that are just forming. This pollen fertilizes the grain. Within it is implanted the germ that will cause it to reproduce. The grain is not the child alone of the plant upon which it grew, but also of the plant from which came the wind-borne pollen that fertilized it.

POLLEN FROM THE TASSEL MUST SIFT DOWN TO THE SILK OF THE EAR OR IT WILL NOT GROW GRAINS OF CORN

With an understanding of these things came the development of independent strains of corn. For generation after generation certain breeders selected their corn and bred toward certain ends. Certain strains that would produce more than other strains were built up. There was much competition among breeders. The pedigree of a given ear of corn came to be recognized as of vastly more importance than the pedigree of a horse that was breaking world records. The corn was producing millions of dollars of wealth while the horse was merely gratifying the admiring tastes of fanciers.

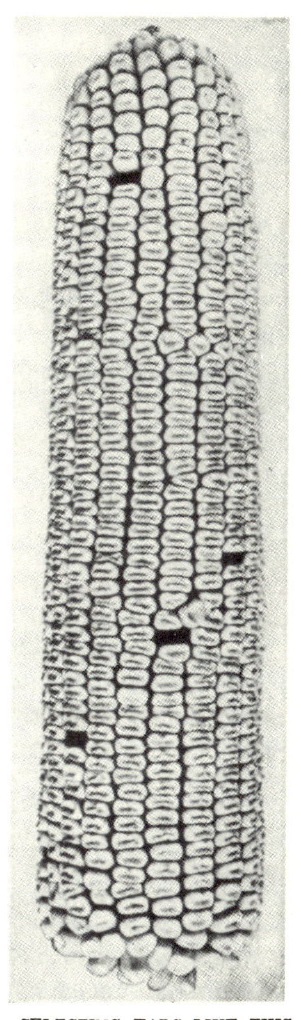
SELECTING EARS LIKE THIS FOR PLANTING GREATLY INCREASES YIELDS

In Illinois, Kansas, Iowa, and many other communities, were developed certain strains that were superior to most others. These were owned by seedsmen who profited greatly by their highly developed strains. And here, again, the Department of Agriculture and state experiment stations found another mistake to set right. The seed that produced the most in Illinois was advertised and sold all over the country. The Department tried it out in Texas, Virginia, and Wisconsin. Perhaps it did well in those communities. Most likely it did not. The climate and the soil of Illinois had gone for many generations into the making of that corn. It was exactly fitted for that climate and soil. It might not fit a different climate and soil. So it was found that the development of a prize strain in a given community could not solve the question for the whole country. A particular strain must be bred for many years in a given community in order to get the best possible results.

The department set out to develop strains fitted to different sections, to get them acclimated and into use among the farmers. It used its influence in inducing the seedsmen and the farmers themselves to do the same thing. Very rapidly, indeed, this is being brought about. The South is at present in need of a developed seed. Only in the last few years has the South awakened to its corn-producing possibilities. It is handicapped until its seed develops. The youngsters in the boys' corn clubs are doing the best work along these lines. They are selling the corn off their plots for five dollars a bushel for seed.

Having thus developed many varieties of very excellent seed, a new plan for increasing the acreage yield has been developed by the scientific breeders. It is a fact long recognized in breeding that a first generation hybrid is often more vigorous for that generation than was either of its parents. In the last few years this idea has been applied to corn. For instance, two separate strains of well-developed seed were cross bred. The seed resulting was planted and the crop obtained was far in excess of the crops of either parent growing under the same conditions. The increase in yield from this first generation hybrid has ranged all the way from ten per cent to ninety-five per cent.

The manner of the hybridization, or crossing, is interesting. Two rows of corn are planted side by side. One row is of one sort and the other is of another sort. They grow up together. When they are getting on toward maturity, the tassels are cut off the corn in one row. That row will then be fertilized by pollen from the other row. The seed resulting will be a cross between the two varieties. When planted, it will yield the large crop guaranteed by the crossing of the strains. The corn resulting from the row from which the tassels were not cut will, of course, pollenize itself and the seed resulting will be the same as the parent stock. But by carrying out this process on the seed plot year after year, the farmer may always plant first generation hybrid seed and always get the consequently large yields. The mistake must not be made, however, of replanting the seed from this large yield and expecting it to reproduce itself, for it will not do so. In the second generation it reverts to the yielding capacity of the parent stocks and to get the continued yields the hybridization must be repeated every season.

The necessity of getting soil in the proper condition, of preventing its exhaustion, of properly fertilizing it, of properly draining it, and of many other phases of soil care, are peculiar to each region and often to each farm. Intelligent thought may solve the given problem in the given places. There are representatives of the Department of Agriculture in every community in the United States. Most of the states have studied the problems that are peculiar to them. Both these authorities have worked out all the problems that are going to present themselves to the farmer. There is no need of his spend-

PLANTING THE SEEDS A LITTLE DISTANCE APART INSTEAD OF CLOSE TOGETHER BRINGS BETTER CROPS

ing years in learning from experience. The farmer should get in touch with these authorities.

There was a time when the government first began to do scientific work for the farmer, that it was not popular. The farmer took the position that he knew his business and needed no help from these men from the cities and the schools. Gradually, however, one after another tried the suggestions that were brought to them and the result was better crops and better profits. In the end all the farmers gained confidence in the scientists.

There is untold wealth in the soil that may be brought forth by the roots of the yellow corn and turned into yellow gold. The men who take the pains to learn the right methods are more fortunate than are those who find the streaks of yellow gold in the sands that wash down from the mountains. Their claims will never be exhausted. The wealth of the Incas and the Aztecs is as nothing as compared with the stores that await them.

CHAPTER VIII

WHERE SUGAR CANE GETS ITS SUGAR

SUGAR CANE is another grass, grown tall. It is a jointed plant with blade-like leaves just as are its modest cousins that grow by the roadside. But man has found that it has a stalk surprisingly full of sweet juice that he has learned to convert into a food called *sugar*. So it has come to pass that this rank grass contributes to the dinner tables of all the world.

Every person in the United States, on the average, eats more than a hundred pounds of sugar a year. Since the average weight of an individual is a little over one hundred pounds, Americans eat something near their weight in sugar every year. Sugar furnishes about one eighth of the nourishment for the human body. The plant that takes the lead in producing sugar, therefore, occupies a place of great importance to man. As a member of the grass family, it is thus related to those other great food crops—wheat, corn, and rice.

It is difficult to comprehend five million tons of sugar but that amount is consumed in the United States every year. If a year's supply of sugar for the United States were loaded on freight cars, they would make a train which would reach from Chicago to New Orleans. The annual supply of sugar for the world would load a train that would reach from Washington to San Francisco and back again.

In the face of the present-day importance of sugar, it is a strange thing to take the back track on it and find out that, as a food, it was unknown in the Italy of Caesar's day.

The story of sugar is a romance which weaves through the centuries. Sugar cane in early days was "the honey-bearing reed" of India. The Orientals said that it was a plant escaped from Paradise. In the Near East it was too young to be mentioned in the Bible, and Buddha, 500 years before Christ, did not know of it. Alexander the Great and his soldiers were the first Europeans to taste sugar. They brought cane back from the Indus, and planted it at the eastern end of the Mediterranean. During the period immediately before the Christian era, the knowledge of sugar spread to China and beyond the Indian Ocean, reaching Java, the sugar bowl of the East, and even extending to the Philippines.

The England of King Arthur never tasted sugar. The Crusaders first encountered it in the East, and acquired an appetite for it. The demand being thus created, European ships went regularly to Tyre for cargoes. From the hot valley of the Jordan sugar cane took its course westward to Cyprus and Spain. Before the time of Columbus, the Portuguese established it on the Azores and the Spanish on the Canary Islands. The sugar crop of these Atlantic islands once dominated the market. The great discoverer planted cane in Santo Domingo, but the West Indian crop awaited the bringing in of slaves before coming into its own. England, even in the time of Queen Elizabeth and Sir Walter Raleigh, had known sugar but now and then. The islands of the West Indies came to be owned by various European nations because each was seeking sugar.

As Java is the sugar bowl of the East, Cuba is its natural home in the West and produces about one fifth

RESIDUE IN SUGAR CANE FIELD AFTER HARVEST

of the world's supply. In those islands conditions seem exactly right for its successful cultivation. It calls for a rich soil, warm weather, plenty of rain, and bright sunshine. Under the right conditions in the tropics, cane grows summer and winter. When it is properly developed for making sugar, it may be cut and a new crop will start at the roots of the old with no need of replanting. Thus one planting may sometimes be enough for the lifetime of the cane grower. In other places the crop may need to be planted every three or four years.

When the crop is planted as far north as Louisiana, where frosts kill it in winter, there is need of great care in ripening the crop and harvesting it before the frost comes. Because of the frost, it is much harder to raise in continental United States than in some of her insular possessions, such as Hawaii or Porto Rico, and in other tropical countries.

There is another plant from which sugar can be made. This is the sugar beet. It will grow in cold climates. Four times as much sugar is made from beets in the United States as from cane. At times Europe has produced nearly half the sugar of the world from beets.

The development of the sugar-beet industry goes back to Napoleon Bonaparte. In the midst of his wars he found that France was cut off from sugar-producing countries and faced a sugar famine. He ordered his men of science to find a substitute for cane as a producer of sugar. The secret of sugar from beets had already been discovered but they developed the methods. The result was that, a little over a hundred years ago, an industry began to be built upon the making of sugar from beets.

In the sugar mill the stalks of sugar cane are passed between huge rollers which press out the juice. This dry cane is then sprayed with warm water and is passed between several sets of rollers. Thus, the last bit of juice is taken out. The impurities are then removed from the juice. It is boiled down to a thick sirup and, under right conditions, crystalizes into sugar.

But the most interesting question about this great industry is, "Where did the cane get the sugar that the factory takes out of it?"

The answer to that question is one of the most fundamental facts in the world. The existence of all plants that grow depends upon it. All animal life, including man, depends directly or indirectly on plant life. They

GATHERING MAPLE SAP TO BE BOILED DOWN

either eat plants or eat other animals that eat them. Sugar is the basic building material of plants. The sap carries it through them that they may grow, bear fruit, and serve their purpose.

Sugar is a carbohydrate. This word means "carbon and water." Stir a bit of powdered coal into water and you have all the elements of sugar though not very neatly put together. Starch is also a carbohydrate. Both these substances are made of carbon, hydrogen, and oxygen. Their only difference is that the materials in them are in a little different proportion.

When the cook wants thick dough for biscuits, she stirs in more flour. When she wants thin batter for waffles, she puts in more water. The plants do the same thing in making starch or sugar. They can change from one to the other at will.

This sugar in the sap of the cane is plant food. It is the basic plant food from which all others are made. It is being carried through the plant to help in the building that comes with growth. The same thing is happening in all plants during their growing seasons. Maple sirup from the sap of a tree is an example of the presence of sugar in sap.

In the plant world, everything depends on the manufacture of sugar. Sugar manufacturing is the fundamental industry of all the world. To grow, every plant must have its sugar factories. From the cradle to the grave, we are surrounded by a multitude of sugar factories. Strangely enough, few of us ever know them for what they are.

Every green leaf is busy all the time making sugar. That is its chief business. It sits in the sun all the time putting carbon, hydrogen, and oxygen together into sugar. This work of the leaves is the greatest industry on earth. It produces the food that is the basis of all life.

The leaf's scheme of manufacture is very well worked out. It has two principle sources of raw material. The first is the water that is brought up from its roots. Water is made of hydrogen and oxygen. There is one raw material yet to be added—carbon. This the leaf takes out of the air. Carbon is present in the air in the form of a gas, carbon dioxide. This is given off when animals breathe or when fires burn. Coal, which is carbon, unites with the oxygen of the air and is changed into this gas. A very small portion of the air, only one part in 3,000, is carbon dioxide. It is injurious to animal life

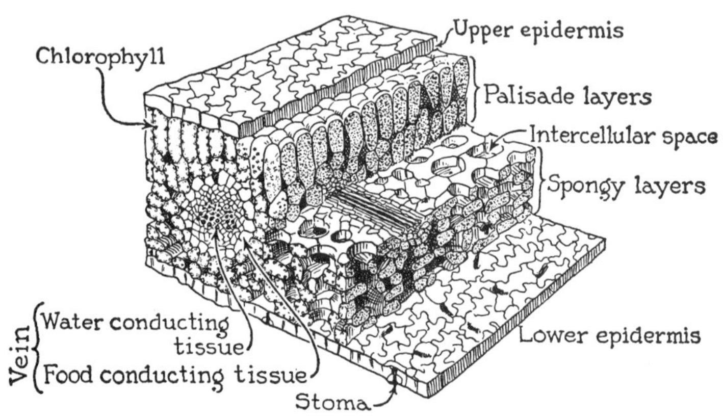

THIS IS THE WAY THE LEAF IS BUILT UP OF CELLS FOR ITS SUGAR MAKING

when it becomes too plentiful. It is what makes the air bad if a room in which people live is not ventilated. But plant life could not exist without it.

About half the weight of cotton, hay, grain, sugar, wood, or any dry vegetable, is carbon. All that carbon has been taken from the carbon dioxide in the air by green leaves growing in the sun.

But man in all his wisdom cannot break up these commonplace materials with which the leaves work and make sugar. With all his research he can only surmise how it is done in the leaves.

He knows that the leaves must be in the sun to do their work. He can put a square yard of leaves in the sun and measure the amount of sugar they make in a day. There will be about enough to sweeten his coffee for breakfast. He can put those same leaves in the shade and he will find that they make no sugar whatever. He concludes, therefore, that the sun helps to make the sugar.

In the sun leaves are green. Put a plant in the cellar and it loses this color. This green coloring in the leaves is caused by the presence of a substance known as *chlorophyll.* It is a hard word but, being the most important substance in the world, one should stop to learn it. This green chlorophyll has much to do with sugar making. It breaks up the carbon dioxide and takes the carbon out of it to mix with the oxygen and hydrogen of water. This carbon dioxide objects to being broken up. It is believed that this green of the leaves has the power of absorbing the energy of the light waves of the sun and of using them in breaking up the carbon dioxide. It is vital to this miracle of Nature's sugar making.

After taking its sugar or starch into the leaf, the plant has a clever way of making it serve its purposes. The chief physical difference between starch and sugar is the fact that sugar will dissolve in water and starch will not. If the plant wants to carry this, its chief food, through its body and branches, it gives it the form of sugar. It will then dissolve in the sap and may be sent where it is needed. When it arrives where a potato is forming on the root of the plant, or an ear of corn is forming on the stalk, it is changed back into starch. It is laid away

COLLECTING THE SAP FOR MAPLE SIRUP

in the potato or the corn as starch and may be kept there for future use. Starch is sugar in stored form.

In coming to understand why plants grow as they do, this sugar-making purpose of the leaf is important. To make sugar, the leaf must expose all the green surface it can to the sun. That is the reason that leaves are broad and flat. That is the reason why a tree sends its branches out as it does in all directions and puts the leaves at their tips. Study the formation of the leaves on any plant and you will easily see that every effort is being made to catch the light rays with their fans.

The long, broad leaf of sugar cane offers much surface to the sun. A field full of these plants, in the bright sunshine, will manufacture many barrels of sugar in a single day. Let that day be cloudy, however, and the sugar production almost ceases. A cloudy spell toward the end of the growing season will have a bad effect on the sugar crop. The world's sugar, therefore, is produced in the lands of bright sunshine.

CHAPTER IX

THE VINE-FAMILY MYSTERY

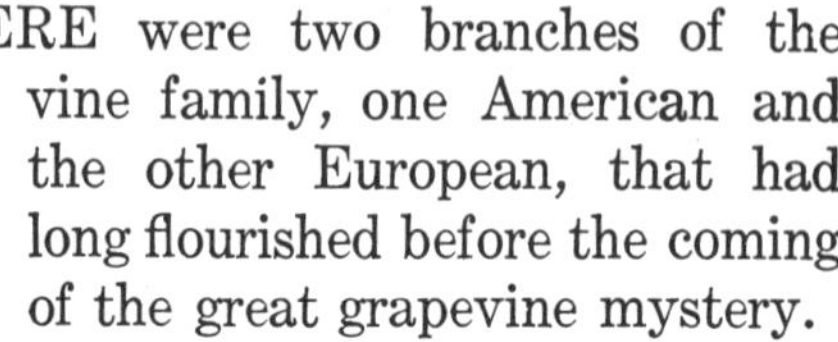

THERE were two branches of the vine family, one American and the other European, that had long flourished before the coming of the great grapevine mystery.

That branch which had made its home in America through the ages had been little in contact with man, had grown unrestrained in the woods, and had offered its succulent globules in the natural state alike to the occasional Indian or the lumbering black bear that came its way.

That branch which had been rooted in the soil of Europe had been long under the care of man. He had tended the soil about its roots, pruned its branches, gathered its fruit for his table and for the making of wine. By selecting the fitter varieties, and by mating those varieties with others of desirable qualities, man developed a grape much superior to those grown at random by Nature.

Yet when this superior European vine was brought to America, seemingly a land which the grape had selected as its own, it languished and died. Imposing colonies of it were planted here and there throughout the eastern states. They were tended by skilful vineyardists brought from Europe for the purpose. The result was always the same—death. For two hundred years these aristocrats of the grape world, coming from France, Italy, and Spain, suffered the same fate. They came to the new land, lived miserably for a season, and died. And those men of many nations who were wisest in the ways of the grape observed and wondered, but were unable to solve the riddle of this tragedy.

PICKING AND FIELD PACKING OF GRAPES

This vine family, from the standpoint of the botanist, we may pause to observe, occupies rather a peculiar position. The vines as we know them, the climbing plants, are by no means all in the vine family. The sweet potato plant and the string bean are vines, but they are not members of the vine family. The vine family in botany is quite dominated by the grapevine.

There are some lesser members of this family, cousins of the grape, such as the Virginia creeper and the Boston ivy, but they are quite overshadowed by their powerful relative. In botany, when we talk about the vine family, we usually mean grapevines.

Almost any plant family is likely to find that it has a vine in it and may be excused if it feels a bit ashamed of this member. A vine, if the truth must be told, is a plant that has lost its backbone. At one time it may have been quite upstanding and self-reliant but it acquired the habit of leaning on a prop and so lost the power to support itself. The wistaria vine, for instance, is a cousin of the locust tree and no longer can stand alone. The strawberry vine sprawls humbly on the ground but is in the same family as the apple tree.

The grapevine is a sturdy sort of plant and one is surprised that it needs to lean upon a support. Yet there it is today, clinging to a dead oak tree or a rail fence or an arbor that man has fixed for it that it may get its leaves up into the sunshine where they may make sugar. It would not have been surprising if students of the vine-family mystery had wondered if this weakness of character had something to do with the failure of the European aristocrat in America.

But despite its lack of independence this star member of the vine-family early made a strong impression on man. Wherever remnants are found of the abodes of early man, grape seeds are likely to be scattered about, showing that they were a part of his scheme of life. It is set down that one of the first things that Noah did when the Ark landed after the flood was to plant grapevines. Virgil, scribe of a dawning civilization, wrote in excellent verse, directions for caring for the vineyard. It is probable that grapes were the first plants that man ever planted near his home and tended to induce them to bear more abundantly.

For 10,000 years, probably, the races from which Europeans came have cultivated the grape. Greece, Rome, France, Spain, have been climes well fitted for its development. It has, therefore, come to pass that the grapevines of Europe are domesticated plants long accustomed to cultivation. It also happens that the grapes have a size and firmness of fruit and cluster, a keeping quality, certain elements of flavor, not possessed by other varieties. They have profited by their long association with man.

Yet the Old World was poor in the possession of grape varieties compared with North America. When Leif the Lucky, and other Norwegian vikings sailed along the coast of New England, five hundred years before Columbus, they gave, as was their way, a picture-word name to the land they saw. They called it Vineland. For America was indeed a land of grapes. It boasts twenty-three species of the thirty or so that exist in all the world.

It was, therefore, not unnatural that European countries, after planting colonies over here, should early think of establishing here vineyards of their improved varieties where the grape grew in such abundance. The London Company, as early as 1619, sent out groups of French vineyardists to Virginia with abundant supplies of European grapevines. The Virginian legislature showed its enthusiasm by passing a law requiring each settler to plant at least ten cuttings. Yet none of these survived for more than a few years. None of these European grapes, to this day, has been grown productively on its own roots in Virginia.

The French Huguenots, a century later, tried in North Carolina and failed. The younger Lord Baltimore planted three hundred acres of European grapes in southern Maryland and none of them survived. William Penn encouraged his Friends in Germantown to grow them but with no results. John Winthrop, Governor of Massachusetts, planted European grapes around Boston Harbor but they died. The Kentucky Vineyard Society, under the guidance of a Swiss, made concerted effort farther west, but failed. Nicholas Longworth, an ancestor of the gentleman of the same name who later became Speaker of the House of Representatives, tried for thirty years to get European grapes to grow in the vicinity of Cincinnati without success. For two hundred years efforts were made in that region, seemingly the natural home of the grape, but everywhere there was failure.

During this time when these same grapes were being taken to Australia, New Zealand, South Africa, South America, even to California, they were growing abundantly and yielding results every whit as good as those obtained in France and Italy. And no man knew the reason for the great American failure.

Then, about the middle of the past century, the curse that lay on the head of the European grapes when they came to America appeared in such a way as to strike terror into the hearts of those millions of people in the Old World who lived by their cultivation. The American curse to the vine appeared in France itself. It came at about the time of the Franco-Prussian War, in 1871, when the enemy captured Paris itself. Yet the defeat at the hands of the Germans was by no means so serious a blow as the blight of the vineyards. It appeared as if this, the major industry of France, were going down to destruction.

EMPEROR GRAPES READY FOR HARVEST

French scientists rose to this emergency and solved the mystery of the blight. In doing so they found out why it had been that European grapes would not grow in America. They found a way to save the vineyards of France from this plant plague. They also found a way to grow European grapes in America. A whole series of miracles of the plant world was revealed.

The defeat of the vineyardists in America through the centuries had been due to the presence of a tiny insect, a plant louse, which the scientists call *phylloxera*. This insect got into the roots of the grapevines and caused them to form galls. These galls were swellings of the roots, hollow inside, in which the insects bred. When they got into the root of a European grapevine, they slowly killed it. These same insects had been killing the immigrant vines whenever they had come to America through the centuries.

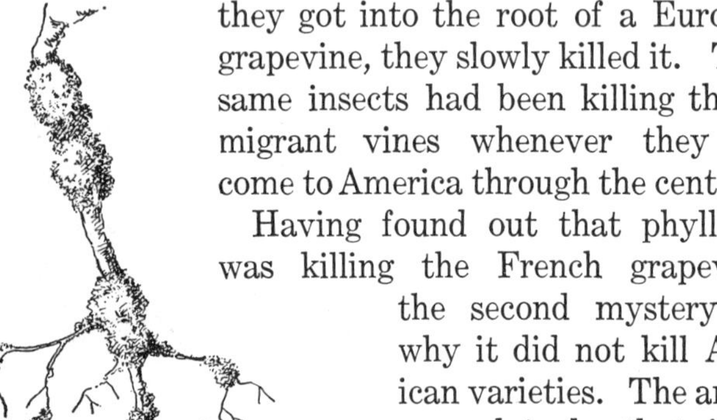

THESE AMERICAN GALLS ON EUROPEAN GRAPEVINE ROOTS ARE SURE TO KILL THEM

Having found out that phylloxera was killing the French grapevines, the second mystery was why it did not kill American varieties. The answer seemed to be that, in the beginning, the insect had existed only in America east of the Rockies. There the vines, having been accustomed to these insects through the centuries, had developed a power to resist them. The European vines, not having lived a long time with the insects, could not survive in the presence of the plague. It was a case like that of the white man who has lived for a long time in the presence of tuberculosis and learned to get on fairly well despite it. When the disease gets among a race which has never had it, however, death occurs with tragic rapidity.

The American grapevines could resist phylloxera but the European vines could not. That fact was established. Upon it the scientists based their whole campaign to save the vineyards of Europe and, incidentally, they showed Americans how they could grow European grapes in the eastern states.

Science already knew how to "graft" one plant on another that was sufficiently close kin to it. It could take the twig of one grapevine and graft it skilfully to the stock of another which had its roots in the ground. The two would grow together. It could, for instance, take an American grapevine growing happily in the garden and cut off its top a foot above the ground. Then it could graft buds of a European grapevine on this stick. The two would grow together.

But the roots of the plant thus built up would remain American while the top would be European.

Since American roots did not mind phylloxera, this plant would grow happily in its presence. Its top, however, would yield the European variety of grapes.

The French saved their grape crop and their wine industry by establishing American wild grapevines in Europe and grafting their favorite varieties on the American stocks. When one rides through France today and sees endless stretches of vineyards, he is not likely to know of the strange wedding of the vines of two continents that has here taken place. But, as a matter of fact, these European grapevines are grown on American roots.

West of the Rocky Mountains phylloxera had not existed in the early days. It was because of this fact that European grapes grew well out there. They had been brought in by the Spaniards and a great industry had been based upon them. The largest grapevine in the world later grew in Santa Barbara County, California. It was planted in 1842 by a Mexican woman. It was eight feet around at the base, covered a half acre of ground, and yielded ten tons of grapes a year.

The insect that blights European grapes also found its way to California. There it has done much damage to vineyards. Many growers have grafted their vines on American stocks, thus saving them by the French method.

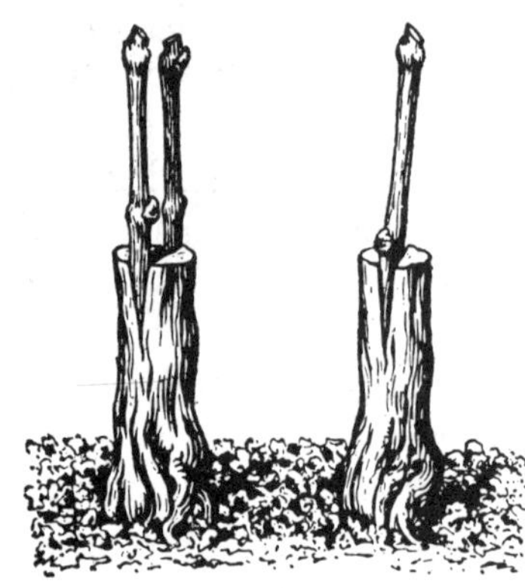
IN THIS WAY THE TOPS OF ONE GRAPEVINE CAN BE MADE TO LIVE ON THE ROOTS OF ANOTHER

While all this history of the European grape was in the making, Americans in the East were experimenting with native varieties and improving them. It is these native varieties chiefly that people who live east of the Rockies have eaten through the generations. Concord grapes are the best known of these varieties. Easterners have acquired tastes for them. They prefer them to those that come from the West, which are European varieties. Those people who have grown up on the Pacific coast, however, have always eaten the European varieties. They regard the eastern grapes as inferior. But when marketmen want grapes that will keep, that will stand shipment, that can go into cold storage and come out good months later, they must select the European varieties. Man, through the centuries, has bred into these grapes those qualities that make them best suited for his purposes.

It has now been nearly fifty years since it was found that Americans could grow the highly developed European varieties of grapes in the East by grafting them on American stock, but they still cultivate the native kinds. It is hard to get away from the habit of centuries. Those who take thought of such matters, however, are aware of the fact that, by getting their plants from intelligent nurserymen, they may grow a variety of European as well as American grapes in a back yard.

There is probably no other plant that will yield such abundant returns in a back yard in proportion to the labor expended as will the grapevine. If it is only thirty feet from the house to the garage and a cement walk runs along the side of the fence, one may build an arbor over that with very little trouble, and convert it into a tunnel of green, bearing abundant fruit. He can set six grapevines in that thirty feet, each of a different variety and ripening at a different time. Each in its season will supply all the fruit that the family can at the time consume. There may be grapes in abundance for months during the summer.

CHAPTER X

THE BAR SINISTER OF THE SUMAC FAMILY

THE Virginia creeper is a beautiful and altogether harmless vine that is cousin to the grape. Like the grape it usually holds on with tendrils. It belongs to the vine family.

Growing beside it in the Middle States is poison ivy which looks something like it, and is often confused with it. This poison ivy, however, is not even related to the Virginia creeper, has no tendrils, and is not a member of the vine family.

It is a sumac, a member of a family many individuals of which seem to have no other purpose in life than to poison and blister whatever poor human beings come near them.

There is a strange group of plants in this family. The ordinary upland sumac is well known, with its sprays of brilliant-colored autumn leaves and its clusters of red berries. It is not poisonous. Its leaves even serve a useful purpose in tanning leather. Then there is the poison sumac that grows in swampy places. It has from seven to thirteen leaflets on its leaf stems, while the upland sumac may have as many as thirty-one. It has waxlike berries, white instead of red.

Then there is poison ivy and poison oak, each of which has the white berry of the poison sumac, a berry a good deal like that of the mistletoe. This white berry is the trade-mark of these three poisonous cousins.

Most of the other members of the sumac family are

POISON IVY HAS THREE LEAFLETS ON A STEM

residents of the tropics. The mango tree is a cousin. So are the trees that bear the pistachio nut and the cashew nut. There is a fruit grown in the West Indies called the Spanish plum, that is produced by a member of this family. The black varnish of Burma comes from a

POISON SUMAC WITH ITS WAXLIKE BERRIES

kindred tree. So do many of the shellacs of the Far East. Strangely there is a touch of the poison in many of these shellacs. A customs inspector at San Francisco once suspected that a can of black varnish of Burma contained opium. In testing it he got a bad case of poison ivy. Some years ago when mah jong, introduced from China, was a popular game in the United States, there was an epidemic of ivy poisoning which was finally traced to the varnish on the mah jong blocks.

Our chief interest in the sumac family lies in the villain members of it. Chief among these are poison ivy which, properly, is not an ivy at all; poison oak which is not an oak; and poison sumac which is often called poison ash and is not an ash at all.

Poison ivy is found over most of the eastern half of United States. In its most familiar form it scrambles over the rail fences and stone walls and grows among the beach sands of Virginia, Maryland, Pennsylvania, New York, and New England. It has smooth, glossy leaves that are attractive to the eye and that take on such brilliant hues in the autumn as to invite picking. The yellowish-green flowers appear in clusters in the early summer while the white, waxy berries cling on after the leaves have fallen in the autumn. It is no uncommon thing to see these poisonous berries sold at Christmas time with greens and mistletoe.

One simple fact serves to distinguish poison ivy from such other vines as Virginia creeper. It has three leaflets on a stem while the creeper has five. There is a homely bit of rime which the country people remember:

"Leaflets three:
Let it be."

There is yet another old-fashioned saying which, if remembered, lifts the ban from the Virginia creeper. It is this:

"Five fingers may handle five leaves."

THE VIRGINIA CREEPER WHICH IS NOT POISONOUS HAS FIVE LEAVES

Poison oak is very similar to poison ivy. It has the same arrangement of three leaflets on a stem. These leaflets are more ragged about their edges than are those of the ivy. This is what gives them the appearance of oak leaves and the plant its name. It has the same kind of blossoms as poison ivy and similar waxy white berries. It is very much like poison ivy except that it grows as a bush instead of as a vine. Both the vines and the bushes are likely to overrun waste places and become tangles four or five feet high.

The leaves of these plants secrete a sort of oil that causes all the trouble. If one's hand brushes against any part of the plant, it is likely to get some of this oil on it. If one's shoe rubs against poison ivy or poison oak leaves, he may get the oil on his hands when he takes off his shoe. He may then rub it from his hands on his face.

Some people are more sensitive to poisoning than others. There are people who can handle poison ivy with their bare hands and not be affected.

When one does get the poison, the trouble begins with itching, followed by inflammation, blisters, scabs, and pus. The irritation may persist for a long time if nothing is done to relieve the condition.

If one knows that he is going out among poison ivy and poison oak, he can protect himself against them. He can take what is called the "iron cure." This is ferric chloride, an iron salt, dissolved in a mixture of water and glycerine. If it is rubbed on the hands and face before they are exposed, it helps a great deal. The iron salt unites with the poison oil and forms a new, harmless compound.

One usually does not know when he is to be exposed to poison ivy, however, and the problem is usually cure

POISON OAK

rather than prevention. Cooking soda applied to the affected parts is helpful. As soon as one can get to a drug store, however, he can buy a simple remedy. This remedy is potassium permanganate. It is a very ordinary and cheap drug. It comes in crystals and, when dissolved in water, makes a purplish liquid. It is interesting to know that these potassium permanganate crystals are also the best known treatment for rattlesnake bite. A few of them rubbed into the snakebite counteracts the poison. It therefore becomes obvious that they are very good to carry in one's pocket when going out among rattlesnakes or poison ivy. They combine with either of these poisons and render them harmless. There are other remedies for poison ivy of which most druggists know. There is no reason for suffering long from its bad effects.

CHAPTER XI

THE GOURD FAMILY

IT TAKES a bit of imagination to think of the cucumber as a gourd. It is hard to say whether it takes more or less imagination to think of the watermelon as one. The cantaloupe of the breakfast table is a closer approach to the gourd form. The squash and the pumpkin are still nearer. All of them, as a matter of fact, are gourds. Then there is the gourd-bearing vine that may scramble up the back porch on which dishrags grow. It, of course, is a true gourd.

The groundwork structure of the plants on which all these products develop shows at a glance that they are much alike. All of them except, possibly, the gourd itself, which often climbs, spread out on the ground. They are all similar trailing vines. They all have broad, hairy leaves with green faces looking up at the sun, busy making sugar. They are closely related plants. They are all in the same family. They are familiarly known as the gourd family but the botanists call them the *cucurbita* which shows where the cucumber gets its name.

These plants are vines but are very different from the members of the grapevine group, which goes again to show that there may be vines in almost any vegetable family. As vines, most of them sprawl out on the ground. This habit proves to the advantage of many of the members of this family. Resting on the ground, they do not have to support the weight of the fruit which they bear. They can let it lie on mother earth, pump nourishment into it, and let it grow as big as it will. Thus it comes to pass that the pumpkin and the watermelon are the biggest fruits in the world. These modest, ground-hugging members of the gourd family challenge the vegetable kingdom to compete with them in the size of the seed cases which they grow.

MUSKMELON (CANTALOUPE)

Gourds proper live chiefly in the tropics though many of them have been brought far north by man and cultivated in his gardens. The bottle gourd vine may climb a tree or an arbor in the back yard. Great beanlike gourds grow from it that may be as much as a yard long. Before man learned to make bottles cheaply out of glass, the necks were cut off these gourds, the insides were cleaned out, stoppers were put into them, and they were used as bottles.

The calabash gourd, a great, tublike fellow with walls an inch thick, was converted by our grandmothers into vessels for holding household supplies. There were gourds for sugar and gourds for fruits dried for winter use. The egg gourd was thinner walled and lighter. It was made into washbasins, egg baskets, sewing baskets, and dippers. The gourd dipper at the well where hung the old oaken bucket was a household utensil in early days. Wherever a spring came from the hillside in our grandfathers' time, there was likely to be found a gourd dipper from which to drink. Gourds were hung in the trees about the homestead in which the martins built their nests. The luffia gourd, eighteen inches long, has a fiber network inside that makes an excellent dishrag or scrubrag for the kitchen and is still often used in place of a sponge in the bathtub. Even banjos and violins were made with gourds as their bases a hundred years ago when people relied on their own resourcefulness for their conveniences. The gourd had its day, but now it is little used except among the poorer peoples.

Cucumbers, which are gourds in a modified form, were among the earliest plants cultivated by man. There are records showing that they were well known in India 3,000 years before Christ. They spread around the world and came to America soon after Columbus. Finally they made themselves the basis of a great pickle industry and got into bottles that sit on the shelves of all the grocery stores of the Western World.

The watermelon is another gourd that has filled up its hollow seed chamber. It is easy to see that it is built on almost exactly the same plan as is its cousin, the cucumber. The vines on which the two grow are much alike.

The native home of the watermelon is central Africa. There are great areas in the heart of the Dark Continent that are overrun with wild watermelons. The natives and the wild animals both feed on this wild fruit. Some of these wild watermelons are sweet and some bitter.

IRRIGATED CUCUMBERS

Whoever would eat wild watermelons must proceed with care. There is wisdom in opening the fruit and tasting it carefully, as the sweet and the bitter are alike to all outward appearances.

The ancient Egyptians cultivated these wild watermelons and, naturally, by selecting only the sweet ones for seed, soon developed varieties that were all sweet. Watermelons were eaten along the Nile in very early times. Pictures found in the older of the pyramids show this.

These children of the tropics have spread all around the world. They like warm climates and sandy soils. They grow best in America in the Southern States. So great has become the industry of raising them that, in

WATERMELON

the United States each year more than 50,000 carloads of them are sent by rail to market. Thus has the jungle gourd vine of equatorial Africa come to bring its fruit to millions of people living all around the world.

"Cantaloupe" is a trade name for the muskmelon, so called because of its musklike odor. Men of science insist on sticking to muskmelon as the name for members of this group. It is the name by which they have been known through the centuries while cantaloupe is only a faddish term to apply to them.

The muskmelon seems to have had its start very long ago in the warmer regions of southern Asia. It has spread all around the world to find its fittest home in the semi-arid regions of southwestern United States where farming is carried on with the aid of irrigation.

THIS PUMPKIN LEAF MIGHT BE CONSIDERED A TRADE-MARK OF THE GOURD FAMILY

The different kinds of muskmelon, such as the Honeydew, the Casaba, the Persian, and the Odessa, are likely to be varieties that have resulted from long cultivation in certain regions. In these days when agricultural explorers travel all about the world in search of plants to grow, all the good varieties are likely to be tried out in a country like the United States. Thus has America come to have many kinds of muskmelons grown in great quantities.

The pumpkin is believed to be a native of America, and to add to that continent's contribution of corn, potatoes, tomatoes, tobacco, and other plants used by man. Yet this is not quite certain. It might be that the Indians got pumpkin seed from some early European explorer and that later visitors thought the plants they grew were native. There are gourds described as coming from the East in early times that might have been pumpkins. Certain it is, however, that this huge cucurbit early found itself a place in the gardens of settlers in America and upon their tables. It was used in making a favorite pie among the early colonists. Since it is at its best in the late autumn, it has become a common food at our national Thanksgiving holiday. Pumpkin pie has become an American institution.

CHAPTER XII

THE ARISTOCRATIC LILY

NO OTHER flower that blows has a place in the religious life and the literature of the Christian world that approaches that of the lily. The glory of the trumpet-like blossom is older than Christianity. The Greeks and the Romans prized it above all flowers, and in their earlier civilizations it had already come to symbolize purity and virtue. It was because of the place it had won in the hearts of these peoples that it found a prominent place in the early paintings of The Virgin and in scenes depicting angels. The Angel Gabriel was accustomed to carry sprays of lily blossoms in early pictures depicting the mother and child, and it is because of this that the most beautiful of these flowers, that most used at Easter, is called the *Madonna* lily. It is also called the *Annunciation* lily for, trumpet-like, it seems to symbolize the spirit of Annunciation Day.

Poets through the centuries have sung the praises of the lily. Phoebe Cary says, "The earth was pushing the cold, dead grass with lily hands from her bosom." "The nunlike lily," says Susan Coolidge, "bows without complaint and dies a saint." Thomas Hood speaks of the lily as "she that purifies the light, the virgin lily, faithful to her white, whereon Eve wept in Eden for her shame." Byron made one of his richest figures of speech when he said, "Her head drooped as when the lily lies o'ercharged with rain." Even Jesus himself never spoke more beautifully than when he said: "And why take ye thought for raiment? Consider the lilies of the field, how

SEGO LILY

they grow; they toil not, neither do they spin: And yet I say unto you, that even Solomon in all his glory was not arrayed like one of these."

Still it is true that lilies, these patricians of the vegetable world, these snow-white flowers that were native through the southern tier of European states, these blooms that have become the flower of France, the fleurde-lis, are but a single member of a great plant family that is far flung around the world and develops many odd relationships.

Strangely the lily is peculiar to the Northern Hemisphere and its temperate regions. Explore almost any north temperate territory and new varieties of lilies will be found. There is a great fellow ten feet tall, for instance, that makes its home in the Himalayas. Agents of the United States Government found a magnificent specimen of lily in northern China a generation ago, a lily of the Madonna type but lustier and handsomer, and brought it to America and have been offering it to citizens from coast to coast. It may displace the Madonna in the course of time.

There are riots of lilies that are native to America. Strangely most of these are radiant with color. There is the Turk's cap, for instance, that is likely to flaunt the deep yellow of its many blooms through the waste stretches between Boston and New York for the pleasure of those who travel that journey in the summer time. Great, stalwart stalks, sometimes nine feet tall, have Turk's caps. They may have half a dozen orange blooms at the top but they who have tamed this plant and given it care have induced it to provide as many as forty blossoms.

A quite different American flower is the little trout lily which likes to grow along the streams or in the deep woods. With the nourishment that it has saved up in its bulb, it starts growing in the early spring and is likely to have bloomed before the leaves of the trees have grown to the stage of making shade to interfere with it. A

ALL THE MEMBERS OF THE LILY FAMILY GROW BULBS

radiant yellow fellow is the trout lily, standing out vividly against its background of green.

Then there is the common wood trillium that would hardly be recognized as a lily. The mottled tiger lily of the Pacific coast has been a favorite for many generations and is reputed to be a different individual from those pure white cousins of the East. In California the "leopard lily lights the heather dun," according to the poet, and the late shorn meadow is often colorful with its bloom.

The red lilies of New England, however, outshine them all and have inspired many a poet of that region. Lucy Larcom spoke of them as "red lilies blazing out of the thicket." Paul Hamilton Hayne thought that the red lily "stands from all her sister flowers apart." Lowell spoke of retreats where "red lilies flaunted." Even the Solomon's seal that hangs its pure white bells along the stem that bears its broad and graceful leaves, is a lily although it has developed on a somewhat divergent plan.

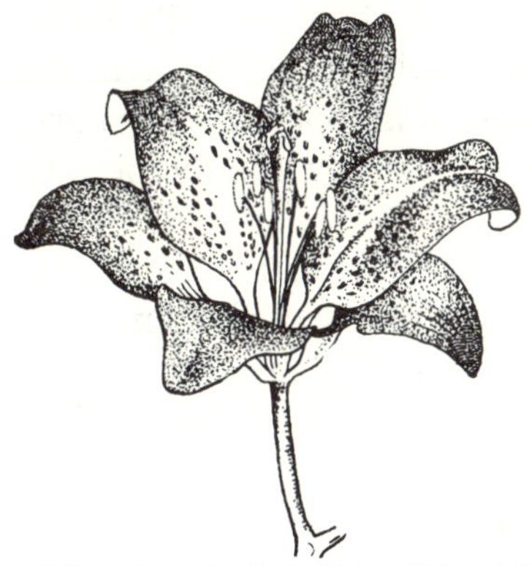

THESE SIX-PETALED FLOWERS ARE TYPICAL OF ALL THE LILIES

Most of the members of the lily family are lovers of damp and shady places. Marshes are likely to be well supplied with them, and even salt water fails to discourage some varieties. They all grow bulbs and bulbs fit more comfortably into loose, damp earth. This bulb-making capacity of the lily family is one of its dominant traits. It and the six petals to all lily blooms are earmarks of the tribe.

Laying down six petals as the symbol in lily land is likely to bring forth a protest from him who thinks of the calla, usually called the *calla lily,* with its single bowl, the flower so often dominant at funerals. Here, the botanists say, a misapprehension has stolen in. The calla is not a lily at all but a member of another family. It is no more a lily than a spider, which has eight legs, is an insect, for the trade-mark of the insect world is the possession of just six legs.

The growing of bulbs to be planted for flower beds used to be an industry a monopoly of which was held by the low countries of Europe. Many of these were lily bulbs. There were also tulip bulbs, daffodil bulbs, hyacinth bulbs, even the modest crocus, that bore the earmarks and were actually members of the lily family because they sprang from bulbs.

Probably the most remarkable lily in all the world, however, is the yucca of the arid plains of the American southwest. Here the lily becomes a plant that is tree-like and that lives on and on through the years. The lily leaves become harsh, dagger-tipped implements for repelling attack. These may sit close to the ground or they may stand as high as a horse's head. From this cluster of leaf-armor there springs now and then a tall stalk that may reach like a flagpole into the desert sunshine. At the top of this staff there forms and finally breaks into bloom such an assemblage of pure white, bell-like, richly perfumed, and in every way perfect, lilies as Nature produces nowhere else in a single cluster. It is given to the desert to grow the greatest of all the lily-bearing plants despite the fact that the native habitat of the family seems to be marshy places.

So far it would seem that this group of plants, that grow from bulbs and put forth six-petaled flowers, serves only

EASTER LILIES

an ornamental and æsthetic purpose in the world and is in no case of any use. This conclusion is far from the mark, however, for there are surprises in store for him who studies relationships in the vegetable kingdom. There are cousins of the lily which, like it, may toil not but which render to man very material crops that find a place on his table at dinner time.

CLEARING OVERRUN BY DAFFODILS

Asparagus is bought in the market tied up in bundles of many stalks, each exactly like the others. There is nothing about asparagus in this form that would indicate that it is a lily. It is such nevertheless. The asparagus bed from which it grows is full of these bulbs that typify the breed. These asparagus tips are only young plants that have just come through the ground. If they were allowed to grow, they would throw out tall, lily-like stalks and crown them with six-tipped flowers that any observer would be able to identify as lilies.

The presence of this commonplace asparagus in an aristocratic family garden is a bit of a let down to its pretentions. This plant, however, is not the worst. There are grosser relatives. There is one lily, rarely thought of as being such, a lowly and useful creature, that offends man's nostrils in the markets of the world.

Going back to the bulb as an indication if not positive proof of the breed, we have evidences that the onion is a lily. Its stalk and flower make out the case. The onion, in fact, is the perfect bulb. It is among the most highly developed bulbs of them all. It is a lily that has been bred through the centuries for the development of its bulb and the suppression of its top. Thus, it has come about that the bulb may be three inches across and the top so insignificant that, when it has dried up, it hardly appears at all. Yet when this top is growing and flowering, it is for all the world like those delicate plants of the window sills which sometimes are called tube roses, but which actually are a delicate, refined, and odorous lily that comes out of the Orient.

Onions came out of the Near East in the dim shadows of the past. The Egyptians pictured them in the pyramids, and the Israelites, wandering in the wilderness, complained to Moses because of their absence. Of the sums expended in the erection of one of the pyramids, according to the chiseled record, there was the account of 1,600 talents spent for radishes, onions, and garlic for the workmen.

Yet even this is not the worst that is to be said of the

plebeian kin of the Easter lily. There is one still more lowly. Garlic, dearly loved by the poor people of the countries that border the Mediterranean, is also a lily. In ancient days it was a staple food of the rural inhabitants of Greece and Italy. Much of the nourishment that sustained the soldiery of those countries in the days of their glory was this same garlic. Not only was garlic a food but it was reputed to have great medicinal value, to be helpful to the stomach in the performance of its functions.

These two bulb vegetables, the Cinderellas of the plant food world, ride about the earth in trainloads and shiploads. Despised as they are, the material service which they render is greater than that of all the other lilies together. The prices they bring in the markets of the world is beyond that of all the other lilies. The sum total of the odors which they give to the world atmosphere is greater than that of all their cousins together, and quite sufficient to snuff out the flower sweetness that typifies the months of blossom time. One would have to look far in all the relationships of Nature to find a contrast more striking than that of the Easter lily and the garlic of the Mediterranean.

Chapter XIII

THE CITRUS FAMILY

IN THESE modern times it seems strange to realize that Rome in her glory did not know of the existence of oranges, limes, or lemons, to say nothing of that infant of the citrus world, the grapefruit, which was developed as a commercial crop in Florida only a generation ago. The romance of the coming to the West of the "golden fruited tree," born in the ancient East where India meets China, of its struggle through the ages to find its home in the tropics all around the world, and its place on everybody's table, is a most fascinating one.

Oranges which are still monarchs of the citrus world, were, in the beginning, of two varieties, sour oranges and sweet oranges. Sour oranges, known also as Seville oranges, are not usually seen in the American market but are much used by the British for marmalade. They spread west from India, swept across the north of Africa with the advent of the Mohammedans, crossed into Europe, and became established in Spain early in the Christian era. They were the only oranges known to the Western World up to about the time of Columbus.

Thus it happened that, when the Spanish first came to America, they brought the seeds of this sour fruit with them. They planted them in Florida and laid the foundation for a great industry. The Indians scattered sour

PICKING ORANGES

oranges among the hummocks where they grew wild as in their native haunts on the other side of the world. So plentiful were they when Florida was later settled that it was long thought that these sour oranges were natives there.

It was about the time of Columbus that the Portuguese, returning from the Orient, brought sweet oranges to southern Europe. It would seem that, where the East Indians had satisfied themselves with sour oranges, the Chinese had developed sweet oranges. Certain it is that sweet oranges came from China and that the Western World did not know them until it got in touch with this land of the East. Certain it is also that many new varieties of them have been brought from the East in modern times.

When Florida came under the flag of the United States, it was found that sour oranges grew wild over most of the state. There was likewise an occasional appearance of wild sweet oranges. The sour oranges were, however, much more abundant. They were also hardier and therefore more likely to survive. They had grown for centuries in Florida and it had become a natural home for them. They fitted the Florida climate. The stock was good but the fruit was inferior. So it came to pass that the sweet orange varieties were grafted on the sour orange stocks. It is from this combination that much of the orange production of Florida has come, although there are conditions where quite different rootstocks are necessary to success.

The Indian River district in Florida was one in which sweet oranges were found growing on the hummocks. An important strain of Florida oranges developed from these wild sweet oranges. As the country became settled, desirable sweet oranges were grafted upon these same sour orange trees that grew wild. They were a great help in forcing the good varieties into development.

A hundred years ago numbers of planted and cultivated groves were to be found in Florida, giving promise of what was to come. Before the United States acquired Florida, Spanish missions and Spanish planters had developed cultivated orchards to supply local needs.

OLD ROOTS WITH NEW TOPS "BUDDED" ON

The first Florida oranges to find their way to any market were raised along the St. Johns River and other streams on which steamboats plied, thus furnishing a means of transportation. This lack of transportation was, of course, the primary obstacle. Half a century ago the chief means of transportation in Florida was by ox team over sand roads where progress was slow. Thus were the early Florida oranges brought to port. They began their journey to market in the holds of ships that were hot, poorly ventilated, and none too swift nor dependable as to time of arrival.

There have been great changes in Florida in half a century. Steamship facilities improved as the population increased. The railroads began reaching into this land of flowers, finally developing into a complete network. Then came those strips of concrete that put wings under the modern, rubber-tired, gasoline-driven vehicles that had displaced the patient oxen. The miracle of the swift-moving truck on improved roads added its most recent contribution. And with these came refrigeration and an organization for handling and broadcasting the crop.

Florida, in the eighties and the nineties, concentrated her citrus efforts on the one product, oranges. The plantings were such, in those times, as to seem stupendous. They went north in trainloads while beholders marveled. There was much talk of overproduction, of glutted markets. By 1895 the crop had actually mounted to 6,000,000 boxes a year. A fruit with which they had formerly had little acquaintance was actually being distributed to the masses of the American public.

Far more important from the standpoint of an original contribution to the well-being of mankind was the development of the grapefruit and its introduction to the public.

There is no more fascinating story of the fruit world than the appearance of this prime favorite of the breakfast table and its growth into favor. So widespread has become its popularity that the present generation is likely to forget that it is entirely new in the world. A generation ago it was known to only a handful of people, to casual visitors to Florida, who were then discovering for the first time that it might be eaten. A generation ahead of that it was sometimes mentioned as a curiosity, the showy but

A WAGONFUL OF GRAPEFRUIT

useless fruit of a West Indian tree. Still further back is the mystery of its origin, for although all the relatives of the grapefruit are known to have come out of the Orient, its exact counterpact has not been found yet and its origin is still a matter of speculation.

The preponderance of the testimony which the government holds points to Barbados as having grown the original plant that is the ancestor of the grapefruit. It seems that in 1696, or thereabouts, an itinerant English sea captain named Shaddock cruised among the ports of the Orient which were then little known. Evidently he was intelligently interested in the strange things he saw. He gathered various seeds of plants that were unknown to the Western World. Then he went on around the world, touching the West Indies on the way to his native England.

Captain Shaddock gave to a friend for planting in the Barbados certain seeds of tropical plants which he had gathered and which, he knew, would not thrive in England. It is probable that from one of these seeds the original grapefruit tree grew. From seeds furnished by this sea captain also came a related plant which bears his name, the shaddock, yielding that huge fruit sometimes weighing twenty pounds but likely to be given to much skin and little meat.

For more than two hundred years the descendants of this grapefruit tree of the Barbados have been grown variously in the West Indies. Different plants under different conditions have developed different qualities. But everywhere the fruit was regarded more as a wonder because of its size than otherwise, and there is no record of any particular value being placed on it as a food.

The written record of the grapefruit in Florida begins with its planting in Pinellas County about 1809 by a

Spanish nobleman. One of the grapefruit trees that he planted is still living, a gallant specimen which stretches out its limbs to a width of sixty feet.

From the grove of this Spaniard, grapefruit trees spread somewhat round about, being grown as ornaments and curiosities because of the great size of the fruit. Through the first three quarters of the last century they were little regarded as an edible fruit. Year after year the heavy crop they yielded fell to the ground and rotted. Nobody had yet conceived the idea that in a little while they were to become the aristocrats among the fruits that graced the choicest tables of the land. They were here and there referred to by writers of the time as late as the eighties as curious but worthless, as not desirable but of showy appearance, as fruit as large as footballs, matters to wonder at, but that was all.

But these Floridians were wise in the cultivation of citrus fruits. They had done much to improve the qualities of their oranges. They applied the same principles to these seemingly useless grapefruit. They found some of them much more edible than others. They selected and developed the better strains. These were scattered among the planters and used somewhat for home consumption. They were offered as a novelty to visitors from the outside. These selected varieties seemed to appeal to visitors. A demand began to be created for them. Some time during the eighteen eighties the first few barrels were shipped to New York and sold at a profit. Shipments trickled north during the ten years that followed, supplying a gradually increasing market. Groves of some extent and of the choicest varieties

THE FIRST NAVEL ORANGE TREE TO BE GROWN IN CALIFORNIA STILL STANDS AND BOASTS A TABLET

began to be planted. The basis was being laid for an industry.

It was in 1895 that the great frost came to Florida, a seeming tragedy at the time, but destined to have a stupendous and helpful influence on the future of the fruit industry and the state.

By killing the tops of the Florida orange trees, it offered a splendid opportunity for extensive grapefruit development. The choice grapefruit varieties had already been well fixed. These grapefruit varieties had only to be

THE NAVEL ORANGE HAS NO SEEDS

grafted on the stumps of the frozen orange trees to turn them into producers of grapefruit. This was done to a considerable extent. The frost also served the purpose of driving citrus fruit farther south where conditions were more favorable to grapefruit production.

The citrus fruit industry developed rapidly in California as that community became settled. There the application of science helped a great deal. The navel orange, for instance, has turned out to be the biggest producer in America. An interesting bit of science is back of the development of the navel orange.

A hundred years ago an orange grower in Brazil noticed a very strange thing about one of his trees. A single branch of it grew fruit that was different from that on the other branches. The fruit on this particular branch did not have any seeds in it.

The owner of this tree took buds from this branch that bore seedless fruit and grafted them on other stock. Thus he grew trees all the branches of which were like this peculiar bud. These trees grew fruit that was without seeds. Thus was the navel orange established. This government found it in Brazil in the eighteen eighties and brought it home and began experimenting with it. It was found to grow well in California where it has become the chief producer of winter oranges.

But there are even stranger facts than these that are coming from studies of plants by scientists, and none is more fascinating than the experiments with the citrus family. A separate chapter will be given to these experiments that show how new fruits may be developed by crossing those varieties that are already established.

Chapter XIV

CREATING NEW CITRUS FRUITS

THE United States Department of Agriculture began working upon the development of new citrus fruits before the past century ended. As a result of its experiments, half a dozen varieties have come into existence that had never been beheld by the eyes of man before the present generation. These new fruits are today being widely grown. Any one of them may tomorrow find itself in use by the people. It was not so long ago that the potato, the tomato, and the grapefruit, were new products of this sort.

In America a hundred years has been spent in developing superior oranges, lemons, limes, and grapefruit. This had been done largely through the constant selection of superior parents for the new plantings. This improvement through selection is still going on and the varieties are being, and will continue to be, improved.

But the government is making a series of scientific experiments much stranger than these and rich in more striking possibilities. These experiments have to do with crossing different fruits in the same family and thus procuring new varieties that have quite different qualities from either parent—in fact, entirely new fruits. The principle is the same as that which is applied when the

THIS IS A NEW FRUIT, HALF LIME AND HALF KUMQUAT

donkey is crossed with the horse to produce the mule. Thus it is that the orange has been crossed with the lemon, the grapefruit, the kumquat, and other fruits, with varying results. Thus it is that most of the members of the citrus family have been experimentally crossed with most of the other members. It has taken decades to find out what the results would be. It looks as if the least to be expected are new fruits that will grow much farther north than the old ones with no fear of harm from frost.

It has long been known that the blossoms of many fruit trees will yield fruit only when fertilized by the transfer of pollen from one to the other. The bees serve as carriers of this pollen. If they should stop visiting from flower to flower for a season, the result would be a complete failure of the fruit crop. When the bee carries pollen from one flower to another, the seed which results is a cross between the two plants on which the flowers bloomed. Plants may thus be cross-bred by placing the pollen of one in the bloom of another.

SHAKING THE POLLEN OF ONE FLOWER INTO ANOTHER PRODUCES A SEED THAT IS A CROSS BETWEEN THE TWO

Man long ago learned how to do away with the services of the bee, and himself cross whatever plants he chose that were capable of being crossed. Plants to cross must be closely related. A paper bag may be put over the flower of a given plant to keep chance pollen out of it, then, at the proper time, the blossom of the plant which is to be mated with it may be brought and the pollen of the one shaken into the flower of the other. From the seeds of the fruit resulting, the cross-bred plants are grown.

One of the early citrus crosses of this sort was decided upon on a basis of common sense. The experimenters conceived the idea that a fruit that was halfway between a grapefruit and a tangerine would be ideal fruit. The grapefruit could not be peeled, could not be divided into segments, was often over bitter, was too big to fill market requirements. The tangerine, on the other hand, was a mild, sweet fruit with a loose skin and easily separated

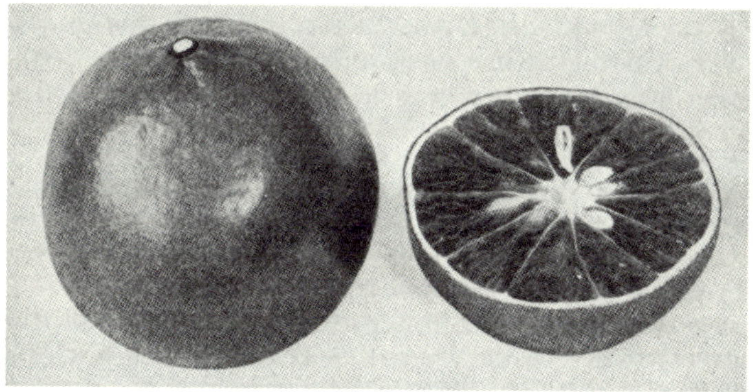

THIS FRUIT IS HALF GRAPEFRUIT AND HALF TANGERINE

segments. It had the additional advantage of not being easily hurt by cold. Could these two be crossed and would the result be a fruit superior to either?

The experiments began at Eustis, Florida, in the early nineties. The pollen of the tangerine was shaken into the grapefruit blossoms. Seeds were planted and nursed to the time of production. The result was fruit of many different kinds, most of which were worthless. It was necessary to select the trees that bore the fruit that was wanted, to raise new generations and again select the best. In the end two varieties were developed that were about right. The scientists gave them a name that is a combination of tangerine and pomelo, which is the proper name for grapefruit. They called them *tangeloes.* Sometimes they are referred to as the squirtless grapefruit. They are bigger than the orange, have the glove skin of the tangerine, lack the bitter partition walls of the grapefruit, have some of the tartness of the one parent and some of the sweetness of the other. They will grow somewhat farther north than will the grapefruit. One of them ripens early and the other in the spring after its competitors have been marketed and it has the field all to itself. These qualities have great possibilities in them. The fruit is steadily growing in popularity. It is as far along now as grapefruit was early in the nineties. There are tracts of considerable acreage now in bearing.

The frost of 1895 had a great effect on the work of the man of science of the Department of Agriculture which followed it. It showed that one of the chief needs of the citrus industry was the development of varieties that would not suffer from frosts in the southern part of the United States.

Out of many experiments and selections came a new fruit the qualities of which have now been demonstrated and which offers a substitute for lemons and limes that may be grown anywhere along the Gulf Coast. This fruit is called a *limequat.* It is a cross between the lime and the kumquat.

The lime is the most sensitive to cold of any of the citrus fruits. It cannot be successfully grown in the

United States except on the southern tip of Florida. The kumquat, native of the Orient, producing that mild fruit little used except for purposes of decoration or for candy, is a vigorous plant that may be grown much farther north.

The limequat may serve all the purposes of lemons or limes. It has possibilities that they do not possess. It has a mild and tasty skin that lends itself to preserving and making candy. It is without the severity of the older acid fruits. But what is vastly important, is the fact that it can be grown with safety throughout Florida.

Such fruits come into use slowly. The demand and the supply must be developed side by side. It is impossible to forecast the caprice of the public taste. It does not, however, seem at all unreasonable to suggest that the probabilities are that the limequat will steadily encroach on the field of the lemon and the lime.

The plant that has contributed most remarkably to cold resistance in citrus fruit, however, is one which yields no edible fruit whatever. It is the trifoliate, or Japanese, orange. It is an ornamental plant that grows in gardens as far north as Washington, D. C. It is a thorny sort of bush, little resembling other citrus trees but bearing a bitter, dwarf fruit in some ways like a tiny orange. It is so unlike the other citrus trees that it has three leaflets on a stem where they have only one leaf. This is why it is called trifoliate.

When experiments were begun in crossing this plant with the sweet orange, there was no great hope of getting a fruit that could be eaten. As a matter of fact, most of the plants that resulted bore fruit that was so bitter as to be worthless. They were promptly discarded. But hybrids have a way of differing in qualities. There was a wide range of fruit on these hundreds of plants. But two or three, however, were mild enough to have possi-

RESEARCH ON LEAF ANALYSIS IN RELATION TO NUTRITION IN CITRUS TREES

bilities. And these were not oranges. They were new fruits with new qualities. They were very acid, more nearly approximating the lemon. They made excellent "ades." Both tree and fruit were beautiful. They were excellent as door-yard fruit. They would grow anywhere through the southern tier of states. The scientists named this fruit, again, after its two parents, the *citrange.*

But the citrange has its faults. Its skin is intensely bitter. Care has to be exercised to keep the skin from getting into drinks made from the juice and spoiling them. It is not a perfect fruit yet. Might not this bitter quality be bred out of it?

Again the idea occurred of crossing this fruit with the mild-flavored kumquat. The cross was successfully made and the wait of years was necessary to measure the result. When the new generation of trees fruited, it was found that some among them yielded a product that had lost much of the bitterness of the skin. The new skins might be eaten or preserved.

This new fruit had qualities not possessed by any others of the citrus group. It was found that by midsummer, while half grown and a brilliant green, it could be picked and used for making "ades." It could be used in that way at any stage of its development. In the early autumn it took on a light lemon yellow. In this stage it was still usable as a substitute for lemons. Continuing to hang on the trees, however, these new fruits, along in the late autumn, would seem to remember that they were descendants of the sweet oranges roundabout and would suddenly take on some of the qualities of the latter. They would turn brilliant orange in color and would sweeten perceptibly.

The scientists called this fruit, from its three ancestors, a *citrangequat.* It is still so new that the possibilities in its cultivation and its adaptation to marketing have not been worked out. Future studies will doubtless develop possibilities that are not now obvious. Some way may be found to extract and transport its juices to market.

Certain it is, however, that this fruit will grow all along the Gulf Coast. It is sufficiently cold resistant to do so. As occasionally happens when these crosses are made, some very surprising qualities attach to the citrangequat plant itself. The citrange plant, for instance, child of two parents so far apart, had certain weaknesses. One of these was that, like most all citrus plants, it is susceptible to canker. The introduction of the kumquat blood into its veins seems to have given a plant that is quite immune to canker, an immunity formerly restricted to the kumquat.

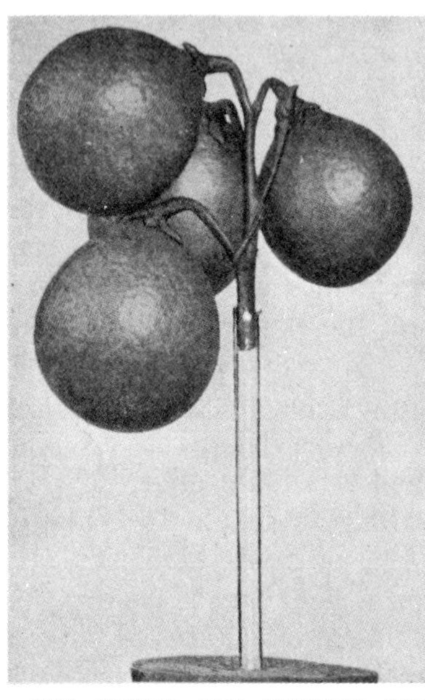

THE ORANGE, THE KUMQUAT, AND THE TRIFOLIATE HAVE BEEN CROSSED TO MAKE THIS NEW FRUIT, THE CITRANGEQUAT

The citrange plant, also, seemed a little confused in its growing habits. If the weather turned warm during the winter, it put out new growth. If it turned cold again, this tender growth was likely to be killed. The kumquat blood in a measure cured this fault. After its introduction, the plant laid dormant during periods of warmth and waited patiently for spring before it did its growing.

No less remarkable was the vigor of the growth of this citrangequat, this mixed-blooded plant. Though the kumquat is a dwarf, its child of a strange cross grew with exceeding vigor. It put forth as much growth in a season as did both of its parents combined.

Because of these physical qualities of this new plant, the citrus growers have found it particularly attractive as a stock upon which to graft various fruits. It is a rapidly growing, cold and disease resistant. These are valuable qualities. The purposes it may serve as a stock are another of the incidental advantages that grow out of these scientific experiments.

These new fruits are cited as mere examples of what is taking place through the efforts of the scientists of the industry and of the government. There have been many other crosses. Many of them are coming along. Undreamed-of fruits may appear this year or the next. A simple cross between a lemon and an orange may yield some new variety that will be superior to anything now in existence. What will a cross between the kumquat and the grapefruit develop? This citrangequat crossed with a lemon may produce a variety of lemon that will be frost proof. An injection of a bit of its blood and a proper selection may bring the citrus belt farther north. There is every assurance that plant breeding will overcome that prime difficulty in the United States, the danger of injury by freezing. Whatever the faults of a citrus fruit and the difficulties of its cultivation, it begins to look as if they might be overcome by the introduction of strains of the proper qualities.

Chapter XV

THE MUSHROOM FAMILY

HERE is a family of pale plants that live in the shade. This family differs from other plants that must have sunshine or they will die. The mushroom, or fungus family, dies in the sun. Flowering plants must spread their green leaves in the sun, that they may manufacture sugar, or they will starve to death. This pale tribe has no leaf green and makes no food as do other plants. It does not need to do so because it steals its food from other plants that have taken carbon dioxide from the air and water and salt from the earth and made them ready for use. The mushroom family usually lives by devouring already prepared food that has fallen into decay. Sometimes, however, it becomes a parasite and lives on other living plants or even in the bodies of living animals. Where it does this, it may become a very dangerous neighbor.

Mushrooms are, primarily, children of the autumn. They are likely to be plentiful on the floors of dense forests after long periods of rain. This is because the plant food in fallen leaves and branches on which they feed is then and there plentiful. The trunk of a dead tree or a fallen log, if the right amount of moisture is present, provides a boundless feast for certain members of the family.

Mushrooms are the scavengers of the vegetable world. They live upon that which is dead and they hurry it on to decay. They have a host of relatives living by the same means, many of which are so small that they are never seen. They help tear down vegetable tissue that has served its purpose. It is largely through them that

CULTIVATED MUSHROOMS

dead vegetation goes back into earth and the air from which it came, that it may appear again in other generations of plants. But for the mushrooms, and the molds that are their relatives, the fallen leaves of the forest would rise about the trunks of the trees and smother them.

These pale plants, living on food provided by their betters, are not very highly developed. They are to trees what creeping worms or garden slugs are to mammals.

The great plant hosts of the world carry on from one generation to another by producing flowers from which fruits develop bearing seed. Members of the mushroom family make no flowers. Their snug umbrellas, however, carry beneath them many ruffling folds and in these develop the germs of mushroom children for another season. Hit a mushroom with a stick when it is getting old and dry, and a cloud of snuff flies into the air. Each tiny particle of this snuff is a spore, and a spore is a seed of a member of the mushroom family. These innumerable spores ride away on the wind and some of them, falling into favorable situations, produce new mushrooms.

The mushroom is the best known of this fungus family. It is likewise among the giants of the tribe. There are various sorts of toadstools, puffballs, coral spots, purple pili, elf-cups, earth-stars, friar's cowls, driad's saddles, and other forms that inhabit any wood. The meadow mushroom is different from that of the forest. Forests of one sort of trees grow different mushrooms than forests of a different sort of trees.

There are likewise many different sorts of molds, and these are cousins of the mushroom drawn to a smaller scale. The mold on the cheese in a refrigerator is a different variety from that on the bread in a box or, again, that which forms a blanket over the jam in a jar. But all are cousins and all are members of this family that loves the dark and lives on borrowed food.

All these plants are fond of damp places and damp weather. If it rains through the weeks of the autumn and the branches of the trees are kept dripping wet, the fungus folk soon begin to appear. Every dead branch, every rotting stump, every bed of decaying leaves, will be covered by some member of this family. With the aid of the dampness and their own secretions, they dissolve the vital parts out of various plant fibers, and the powder that is left goes back into the soil. Thus do they serve their purpose.

These agents of plant decay, unfortunately, have never learned that logs in a barn and rails in a fence are serving man's purpose and therefore should not be aided in the processes of rotting. The mushroom brood attacks them also and does much harm to man's structures. There are certain of them that, becoming parasites, fall upon man's planted crops and destroy them. There are microscopic members of the family called *bacteria,* plants that attack man's vitals and cause him to die. Bacterial diseases are caused by plants just as germ diseases are caused by tiny animals. There are harmful bacteria and beneficial bacteria. Much more is made of the members of this family that are hurtful to man than is made of those that are helpful.

There are many commonplace diseases that are caused by a fungus that attacks the human body. Ringworm, it happens, is not a worm at all but a plant growth beneath the skin. Barber's itch is another skin disease of plant origin. So is trench foot, which was such an irritation to the troops during the war.

Since it is the nature of fungus plants to like low temperature and acid rather than alkaline conditions, not many of them attack the higher animals. Cows and their fork-toed cousins are given to having "lumpy jaw" as a result of a plant growth inside them. As one goes down the scale of domestic animals to the lower orders, the damage is greater. There is that modest and productive domestic animal, the silkworm, which was among the first to be fitted to the purposes of man. It is quite

MUSHROOMS GROW IN FANTASTIC SHAPES

subject to fungus attack. There have been times when the industry was threatened by it. Many insects have their destructive plant enemies and the government often makes use of this fact. If an insect becomes a plague, the government may hunt up a plant parasite and set it upon the troublesome pest and thus destroy it.

Fungus attacks on plant crops are often costly to man. In the United States, there are a number of them that have been battled by the government for years. There is, for example, the apple rust which, in some sections, often destroys the crop.

This apple rust furnishes a striking example of the manner in which a member of this fungus family, a cousin to the mushroom, that has formed the habit of living on live plants, proceeds to do vast damage. It all begins with the cedar tree. Who, in examining a cedar tree, has not noticed the little, round, gall-like balls that form on its twigs? Yet who would have surmised that these balls might be responsible for the blight of the apple crop?

These galls are formed by the presence of a fungus plant. It is because of this fungus that the twig swells and forms this hollow ball. It is inside this ball that the spores which are the seeds of this particular fungus plant develop. They are of the same sort of snufflike spores that the mushroom develops in the ruffles under its tent and which fly away on the wind if you hit a dried one with a stick. They are very tiny, these spores, and very light. There are millions of them in a single gall. When they are ripe, the gall breaks open and they start on their journeys. They may go but a few hundred yards or they may travel for miles. What they are looking for is an apple tree. They will live on no other sort of plant. If they do not find it, they will die. If they do find it, they settle down on its leaves and increase from a few individuals to multitudes. In this new stage, fed on this new food, they take on a quite different appearance. They become the rust which saps the strength of the tree and destroys the crop.

It is a strange thing that the fungus that develops into the apple rust must live for one part of its life on a cedar tree and the other part on the apple tree. It can keep alive on the apple tree only while the leaves and fruit are green and tender. It requires that sort of food for its summer fare. But its winter diet and its nesting place are in the twigs of cedar trees. Apple orchards, therefore, will suffer from rust only where there are cedar trees near by. Consequently, in the apple country, where there is trouble from the rust, the best thing to do is to cut down the cedar trees near by.

AN EDIBLE MUSHROOM

The black stem rust is a fungus disease of wheat. It is a living plant that attacks the wheat fields. White pine blister is another of these fungus parasites that sets out to see how much harm it can do. Soft little cousin to the mushroom that it is, it will walk right up to a huge white pine tree, grapple with it, and, strange as this may seem, will do it to death. It is then not satisfied with its work. It will spread to the white pines roundabout and kill them all. It will wipe out whole forests of white pine. Then it will ride away on the wind to another such forest and do it to death. When once it gets started on so large an area as a continent, there is need of putting up a stiff fight or white pines may disappear.

The United States Government is just now fighting the white pine blister in an attempt to keep it from destroying all of this variety of timber between Maine and Oregon. The fight has been on for years in the East. The government had established a dead line at the Great Plains and had hoped to hold the plague to the East. It was successful for years, but the Canadian Government was not so vigilant. The blister got through the Canadian forests and, paying no attention to border guards, walked right into the United States by the back door.

This pine blister spends one part of its life on its favorite forest tree and another stage on a quite different vegetable host, on the currant bush, or on its cousin, the gooseberry bush. Currant and gooseberry bushes are not important in the timber country, and the government would gladly sacrifice them all to get rid of the menace to the pine trees. They grow wild, however, and digging them all up is a task that is next to impossible. But such is the method of campaign in this particular warfare.

It is strange that these pale little plants should be so hard for man, organized into the strongest government in the world, to cope with. Yet as plants go, the fungi, low order that they are, are probably man's most desperate and effective enemies.

Chapter XVI

LESSER GARDEN RELATIONSHIPS

IF ONE should go into the vegetable garden and try to pick out the plants that are related to each other, he would be likely to make many mistakes. What would be more natural, for example, than that he should conclude that lettuce, which often develops compact heads, is a close cousin to the cabbage?

As a matter of fact, these two plants are not in the same family at all. Cabbage is a mustard, while lettuce, strange to say, is a member of the sunflower family. It is a cousin to the daisy of the meadow. It may be easier to see that it is kin to the dandelion of the lawn. Dandelions, in fact, are sometimes grown in gardens for greens.

If lettuce were allowed to go to seed, its kinship to these other plants would be easier to see. It will be remembered that they are all composites—their flowers are all made up of many small ones bound together in a circular group.

As long as man has been able to write, he has mentioned lettuce as food. He doubtless began with some plant related to the dandelion and, by selecting those with better leaves and solider heads for planting through the ages, steadily improved the quality of his salad.

Cabbage, which belongs to the mustard family, probably got its start in a similar way. The mustard plant grows wild and waist-high in many parts of the United

States. Its straggling leaves are much like those of the cabbage. But the cabbage was bunchier and closer to the ground. Wild cabbage plants still may be found on the chalk cliffs of England. Man has kept breeding them to get a solider head. The cabbage has come to be cultivated more and more until it is now grown all over

CABBAGE IS THE MOST IMPORTANT LEAF CROP

the world. It is the most valuable of all the leaf plants and goes in boatloads and carloads to all the populous centers.

While cultivating the cabbage in his garden, man has, from time to time, noticed odd individuals that had certain differences from their fellows. There were certain cabbage plants, for example, that grew rows of buttons up and down their stems. These buttons were like tiny cabbages and the Belgians noticed that they were tender and delicious. They began selecting the plants that grew these tiny cabbages and developing them. In the end they had a breed of cabbages that gave most of their attention to these buttons on their stalks. They came to be popular in gardens and were given to the world as Brussels sprouts, so named after the capital of Belgium.

The cauliflower is another offshoot of the cabbage. It is not the leaves but the bloom that here attracts attention. The word means, literally, "cabbage flower." The cauliflower is a swollen and distorted cabbage bloom. It was found to be good to eat; consequently gardeners have developed a race of cabbages with swollen blossoms.

One might think offhand that turnips, beets, and carrots were relatives because each has a meaty root in the ground which is its most important part. Each is a two-year plant. Each uses this root as a storehouse for food in the same way. Each sends a tuft of green leaves up into the sun where, during the first year, they busily manufacture sugar to be stored as food in this meaty root, for use in sending up a stalk the second year which feeds on it, blooms, and makes seed. But this is not a trick that indicates kinship. It will be remembered that the bulbs of the lily family do the same thing. Turnips, beets, and carrots are each of a different family.

The turnip is closely related to mustard and the cabbage, which plants have no storehouse at their roots. The radish is another vegetable that belongs in this mustard group. The beet, however, is a member of the goosefoot family. Man long ago noticed its tendency to develop a root that might be eaten, and started in to develop this root. The beet of the family vegetable garden is one result. It was found that there was much sugar in this beet. During his wars, Napoleon found that his sugar supplies from his West Indian colonies

LETTUCE IS A COUSIN TO THE DANDELION AND THE DAISY

were cut off and so he ordered his scientists to find some plant that could be grown in France from which sugar could be made. They learned that it could be made from beets. That started the development of the beet along a different line. Now sugar beets that weigh fifteen or twenty pounds each are grown. They produce many tons to the acre and yield much sugar. They are grown in such quantities as were never dreamed of by the modest little beet of the garden.

There is a close relative of the huge sugar beet, growing in gardens, which has no storage root at all, and finds its way to the dinner table in a very different form than sugar in the bowl. Spinach is a goosefoot, first cousin to the beet. Eating spinach, the doctors say, is one of the easiest ways to get iron into the blood. These leaf vegetables, in fact, are rich with earth minerals and salts which the human system demands. One is much healthier for having them in his diet.

In looking for relationships in the garden one might hit upon celery and rhubarb as showing traits of kinship. Here are two watery stalks of a seemingly similar nature that man has come to use as food. It is the stem of the leaf that man eats, not the leaves and the roots. In each case a plant has been found that grew large leaf stems. Man has developed this peculiarity into a vegetable of value.

But these plants are not related. Rhubarb, strange to say, is a member of the buckwheat family, oddly astray in our gardens. Celery, on the other hand, is a cousin to the carrot which was denied admission into the families of the beets and turnips, rooty plants like itself. Celery is a member of the parsley group. The carrot is a root plant. Celery emphasizes the leaf stem. Man has taken advantage of the tendency of each and profited by doing so. The wild carrot grows throughout much of the United States. It is like the cultivated carrot except that its root is smaller. It furnishes an excellent example, however, of just what can be accomplished by breeding a wild plant. In many cases the wild plant has been lost and cannot be compared with the cultivated plant. Here, however, both may be seen.

Celery, the cousin to the carrot, is one of the marvels of the vegetable world. Its huge leaf stems, in an economy of Nature, would hardly seem necessary to support the tiny tufts of green at their ends. They have, in fact, been coaxed into an abnormal growth so that man might crunch them at dinner time. At the beginning of

CELERY IS A CARROT WHOSE LEAF STEMS HAVE BEEN DEVELOPED

the present century, celery was almost unknown as a commercial crop, and was little grown except in the home garden. Then farmers began to learn that great quantities of it could be grown on an acre of land and sold profitably in the big markets. California, Florida, the Great Lake Region, New York, and New Jersey, went into celery growing. In all those regions it is no unusual thing to raise $2,000 or $3,000 worth of celery on an acre. Crated celery began to go to the cities in carload lots. By 1925 some 20,000 carloads a year were being produced. It would take a string of freight cars 200 miles long to haul the present annual output of the swollen stems of this member of the parsley family.

There is an odd link between the vegetable garden and the flower garden, due to family relationship. The purpose of the vegetable garden is usefulness, of the flower garden, ornament. The sweet potato is an important product of the vegetable garden. It stores up plant food on its roots for one year to provide a good start for the crop of the next year. On his first trip to the West Indies, Columbus found that the natives were taking advantage of this stored plant food and turning it to their own uses as food. Sweet potatoes had been unknown in Europe up to that time, but Columbus took them back with him and they began to spread all over the world. They have come to be one of the crops that yield most abundantly in proportion to the amount of labor given them and therefore are one of the cheapest of food crops.

There is a cousin to the sweet potato in the flower garden. It is none other than the morning-glory which blooms forth to meet the sun and then closes up its flower by the time the dew is off the grass and the ants are out hunting honey. One would not be likely to think of a relationship between these two plants, but when he compares them the vines and leaves are so much alike that it is obvious.

Although these vines are so nearly alike, each lacks the peculiar feature that is the most notable quality of

ONCE IN A WHILE A SWEET-POTATO VINE BLOOMS AND SHOWS ITS LIKENESS TO THE MORNING-GLORY

the other. The morning-glory has no potatoes on its roots, stores no food whatever, as does the potato. On the other hand, the sweet potato usually makes no bloom, and it is upon its flower that the fame of the morning-glory rests.

The sweet potato was doubtless at one time a flowering plant like the morning-glory. It still blooms in the tropics. On some occasions in its life history it doubtless found difficulty in keeping itself alive through flowers and seeds. Plants have great powers of adaptation that they may survive. The sweet potato, for example, turned to storing food at its roots and sending out sprouts from these food sources for the next crop. This worked better than flowers and seeds, and the latter were gradually abandoned. In the North the sweet potato makes no seed.

The morning-glory, however, holds to flowers and seeds. Anybody who watches one of these vines through the season will observe the compact little ball of seeds that follows the flower. Then, in the autumn, these seeds rain upon the ground under the vine and insure a crop for the next year.

Now and then a peculiar thing happens in the sweet-potato patch. Occasionally, in the North, a sweet potato vine will put forth a flower. When it does so, that flower is one of the true trumpet variety, very much resembling the morning-glory and thus furnishing an additional proof of the relationship between these two vines.

Chapter XVII

THE PALM COUSINS

HE palm tree is an odd sort of fellow when compared to the pine tree, the oak tree, the apple tree, or any of those other monarchs of the forests that "lift their leafy arms to pray." It is different from them in so many ways that one naturally concludes that it belongs to a group which is not very closely related to them.

In the first place, it differs in the way it grows. It starts out by being a great spray of leaves appearing above the ground. As it grows the first of these leaves spread back flat on the ground and others unfold from the center. Leaves, it seems, keep pushing up from below. Layer after layer of the old leaves die. New ones take their places above them. Each adds its mite to the height of the trunk of the palm.

A strange thing about this trunk is that it is as big when the tree is young as it will ever be. Take a palm tree the trunk of which shows only a foot above the ground. The trunk is as big around as it will be when the tree is a hundred years old and a hundred feet high. The palm tree finishes its structure inch by inch as it shoots up. The method, of course, is quite different from that of the other trees whose trunks grow bigger and bigger with the passing of years.

The palm tree, as a matter of fact, grows only at one place—its very top. At that top new leaves are always forming. They always look like a huge bud that is getting ready to open, or like a cabbage. This tip of the palm tree is in fact sometimes called the cabbage. In some countries it is cut out and eaten. This of course kills the tree.

The secret of this strange manner of building up the palm tree is the fact that it is an inside grower, while most trees are outside growers. The sap of the oak tree flows up through channels created for the purpose between the bark and the body of the tree. The sap carries the building materials from which the leaves, twigs, and branches are constructed. Every year it puts on a new layer of wood growth on the outside of the trunk itself. The trunk thus grows bigger every year.

But in the case of the palm tree the growth is through the inside. The sap comes up through the middle of the tree and piles all the building material into the leaves in the cabbage. The hard shell of its trunk, having once taken form, never changes. With trees that are cared for by man, the dead leaves are likely to be taken away, but in the wild state great bunches of them cling to the stalk.

Some of the other families which we have studied grow in the same way. The grasses, for instance, are inside growers. The manner of their growth may be seen by examining a tiny blade of grass on the lawn or a stalk of corn in the field. The leaves come out of the center and unfold. The stalk of corn is as big around the bottom

CABBAGE PALMS GROWING WILD IN FLORIDA

when it is a foot high as when it is ten feet high. Its leaves cling to its trunk as do those of the palm, and the lower ones die in the same way.

Any of the bulb plants that grow readily in the garden or in a bowl in the window are also inside growers. They are not members of the grass family but of the lily family which is closely related to it. Onions and asparagus belong to this family. They may be observed in any garden, growing only at the top.

The grasses, the lilies, and the palms, therefore, are three distinct families which form a group with certain common characteristics. In a way the palms are grass trees. Their leaves are bladelike as are those of the grasses and the lilies. Their flowers appear in sheaths and open up into branching spikes that are likely to be a good deal like the tassels of corn or oats. The three are distinct families, yet related.

Palms divide themselves into two classes through the different appearance of their leaves. These are the feather palms and the fan palms. The leaf of the feather palm may be ten feet long with blades branching out all along the stem as do the ribs of a feather. The form of the fan palms is plainly demonstrated in the palm leaf fan, so useful in the summer time.

Most of the valuable members of the palm family, such as the date palm and the coconut palm, are feather palms. The palmetto, a dwarf American palm, is a fan palm. So is the magnificent Washington palm which is a native of California and rears itself so proudly along many an imposing driveway of the Southwestern States.

It was probably from these fan palms that this plant family took its name. The leaves of the fan variety spread out like the fingers from the palm of the hand and thus, doubtless, suggested the idea to the early name makers.

COCONUT PALMS GROWING IN AN OLD PLANTATION

The palm tree has always held a high place in the estimation of man and has exerted a strong appeal to writers and artists. It was early called the "prince of the vegetable kingdom," although its structure is simple and it actually deserves no such high rating. It presents itself in many varieties all around the world in tropical climates. It shows how different members of a single family can be, for instance, when it presents the stalwart Royal palm of the Florida Keys, and the rattan canes which are spindling plants that cling like grapevines to forest trees for support.

There are two members of the palm family that stand out above all others for usefulness to man. These are the date palm and the coconut palm, each furnishing food for millions, each a feather palm, yet with fruit so strangely different and with life habits as unlike as they well can be.

The date palm was one of the first plants ever cultivated by man. It probably developed around the Persian Gulf in the torrid south of Asia. The Shatt-el-Arab River flows into this gulf from the north. It is but seventy miles long and is formed by the union of two historic streams, the Euphrates and the Tigris. It is bordered for its entire length by date orchards. Its bottom lands may be irrigated easily from the river and every available inch is planted in dates. The plantings extend up the Euphrates and the Tigris. Arabia is a sandy desert with a fertile oasis here and there. These oases, some of them quite lost in the solitudes, are given over almost exclusively to the cultivation of dates. These dates are the chief support of the Arabs. Thousands of tons of them come down to the coast every year, reach the channels of trade, and spread out to all the world.

Dates will ripen only where it is very hot and very dry. They must have their feet in moist ground but their heads in the burning sun. Long ago they crossed over the Red Sea into Egypt and from there to the oases of the Sahara. Here they became the chief product of those wet spots in an otherwise bone-dry area. They crossed over to Spain where their cultivation was only partially successful. The date palm will grow in southern Europe and in many American states but, because of the presence

DATE-BEARING PALMS NOW GROW IN THE UNITED STATES

of moisture in the air, they fail to bear fruit. Thus, it is a wisp of date palm that one is likely to wear in his buttonhole on Palm Sunday.

In the American Southwest, in Arizona and California, areas have been found that are very dry and hot, moisture being furnished by irrigation. Here the date has been planted and prospers. Here science has been applied to the peculiar problems of this desert plant, and it is beginning to appear that America may come to raise commercial dates that are quite superior to those of Arabia, the date mother. Date farmers in the Imperial Valley, for instance are getting twice as much food value from an acre of dates as can be coaxed from an acre planted to corn, and are finding the new crop profitable.

MALE AND FEMALE FLOWERS OF THE DATE PALM

There are those who hold that man's first application of science to agriculture occurred in his cultivation of date palms. He early discovered that there were male trees which produced blooms but no fruit, and female trees which bore fruit. The male trees took up half the room in the orchard and therefore cut down the yield. Doubtless some Arab long ago got the idea of cutting out the male trees and planting females in their places. If he carried this scheme too far, if he cut down all the male trees, he found that even his females ceased to produce and his orchard was barren. Doubtless this early Arab was much puzzled. Nobody knows how many centuries it took him to find out that female flowers had to be fertilized with pollen from male flowers before they would bear fruit. But in the end he did find this out about 6,000 years ago. He worked out a scheme for making the female flowers fertile without giving up half of his orchard space to male trees. Ancient pictures in the pyramids show details of this process.

One male tree is planted to every 50 or 100 female trees. The buds develop in great sheaths and break out into blooms that look not unlike giant corn tassels. In the natural state, the male flowers give off pollen which floats in the air and reaches the female flower. When there is but one male tree to fifty females, however, there is not enough pollen in the air to fertilize the orchard in this way. The early Arabs found that if they would break off a sprig from the male flower and bind it to a female cluster it would furnish enough pollen to fertilize that cluster. One male tree would provide enough sprigs for 50 to 100 female trees. By taking a bit of pains in this way the orchards could be so handled that only an occasional barren male tree was necessary. All cultivated date orchards are treated in this way. They have been so treated for many thousands of years. In this way a knowledge of some of the secrets of Nature is shown to extend far back into the past.

With the coconut palm, all this is different. Instead of being a child of the desert it has, through the ages, been a lover of tropical beaches. It finds its favorite home in the many islands of the Indian Ocean and the South Seas. It is partial to the strips of sand that border the ocean. It takes root in this sand and starts building up its trunk with the tuft of leaves at the top. Unlike most palms its stalk may be crooked or leaning. But it keeps going up until it may be 60 or 70 feet to where the coconuts hang.

The coconut bloom is a good deal like that of the date. It is different, however, in the fact that both male and female blooms occur on the same tree. There are no male and female trees as in the case of the date. Each cluster of flowers fertilizes itself.

It is strange that these two trees, so much alike in general structure, should have developed fruit that is so unlike. The meaty little date with its pitlike seed does not bear much resemblance to the huge coconut surrounded by its grizzly wrapping

The differences in the fruits of these two palms is an excellent example of the manner in which plants will adapt themselves to different surroundings in order to survive. The date, growing in a narrow valley, found that it could best get itself planted if it presented a small seed surrounded with a sweet meat. This would induce man and other animals to carry this seed away that they might eat the meat. Then the seed would be thrown down and might take root and grow.

The coconut was faced by a quite different problem. It grew on the beach of a coral island of the South Seas. It wanted so to develop its seed that it would have the best possible chance of finding a home somewhere on some similar beach. If it was to find a new home, its best chance was by floating to it. So the coconut developed a huge hollow seed which floats. But it found that

THE COCONUT PALM WITH ITS LAP FULL OF FRUIT

it must put in a meaty food supply for the young plant to live upon while it was getting started in life in the sand. This made it heavy and dragged it down despite the fact that it was hollow. Then it built a fibrous husk about its nut that would stand much knocking about and that would help in the business of floating. In the end it developed a huge, cushioned nut that was nearly a foot long.

The coconut palm, leaning out from the beach, might drop this fruit into the waves of an outgoing tide. That tide might carry it far to sea. It might float about the ocean for many months. It might, in fact, float there until it decayed and disappeared without ever finding a chance to grow. But, on the other hand, the waves might some day cast it upon the beach of some new island. There it might find its opportunity. It might take root and grow. It might become a palm tree that would produce these huge nuts in new surroundings. It might start a new colony of its kind. It was for this reason that its parent tree had developed it into this peculiar form.

This, then, is a new evidence of the wisdom of Nature. What if the coconut palm tree had put all its female blooms on one tree and all its male blooms on another as did the date palm? When this coconut found its new home and grew, it could not have produced fruit because it had not brought a companion tree with it to supply the pollen. Each tree, in fact, has worked out its scheme of life in a peculiar adjustment to the place in which it lives.

And how useful has this coconut palm become. The half inch of meat with which it lines its shell that the young plant may have food has become a most important item of commerce. Everybody knows the coconut as it may be bought in the market, cracked open and eaten. Everybody knows the shredded coconut of the kitchen that so often appears as part of the candy he buys. This, of course, is the meat of the coconut in a prepared form. In coconut land a great industry is based on the gathering of this fruit of the palm and the separation of this meat from its other parts. This meat, dried and ready for market, is called *copra.* It is the raw material for many products. The public knows little of the greatest of these products—coconut oil. Copra is fifty per cent oil which may be recovered by running it through a press. This oil is a white fat of which many uses can be made. It is, for instance, converted into butter substitutes which many people eat without ever knowing that it does not come from a cow. As the animal fats of the world decrease, there is a bigger and bigger demand for this vegetable fat. Thus is a mammoth industry developing. There are places in the world where huge plantations, containing as much as 100,000 acres, are being planted to coconuts because of the increasing demand for vegetable fats.

The towering individual palm of some of these plantations is a most admirable specimen. It may rear itself fifty to one hundred feet high. Its huge sprays of flowers appear from the base of its lower leaves. One of these bunches may produce from ten to twenty coconuts. A single tree may have a dozen bunches. A hundred coconuts is an average yield for developed trees. There is a prize tree in the Philippines that has produced as many as 470 coconuts in a year.

This is the most useful of the palms. The prospects are that it will grow steadily in importance with the passing decades.

CHAPTER XVIII

COTTON OF THE MALLOW FAMILY

NOT much would ever have been heard of this plant family had it not been that one member of it developed a peculiar trait that fitted into man's scheme of making use of plants. The mallows are mostly scrubby shrubs and bushes that grow in the tropics, some of them becoming important enough to rank as trees. There is the marsh mallow, for instance, which produces the material that is often found in candy. And then there is the cotton plant. It was this cotton plant that had a certain peculiarity which made it and its whole family famous.

The strange thing which this cotton plant did, came about as another of that multitude of tricks played by plants which want to get their seeds planted. It put fluffy fiber about its seeds to give them wings. Those cotton plants that merely put their seeds in a pod and dropped them did not spread far. Tying fibers to their seeds was the old trick of the dandelion in a little different form. These fibers caught the wind and helped the seed to ride away to a new plot in which to grow. They bundled the seed up in such a way that it might the better be kicked about. They made it float or sail farther than if it fell in the water. The cotton plants with hairy seeds got along better than the others. Those without hairy seeds tended to die out. So cotton plants raised hairier seeds until, finally, they were established as plants with hairy seeds.

As man advanced in the world, he learned to make one and another of the animals and plants about him serve his purpose. The skins of animals were doubtless his first clothes. The mild-natured sheep came early to live with man, and before long he had learned to twist its wool into yarn and weave cloth from it. It is probable that the first cloth was made of wool. Then the Chinese learned to spin silk from the cocoons of silkworms. Silk was known before cotton. Silkworm culture was known in Europe earlier than was cotton. Flax was used in Egypt and along the Mediterranean for cloth making long before cotton. Then in India, probably 5,000 years ago, cloth began to be made of cotton. It has been found, by digging in the ancient ruins of Peru, that the people who lived in the Andes made cotton cloth even before it was manufactured in India. The quality of this cloth was excellent. The Pueblo Indians, in what is now New Mexico, grew cotton and made blankets of it.

COTTON READY FOR PICKING

It would seem that the use of cotton got started in both India and America a long time ago.

In America we think of the cotton plant as a field crop that grows only three or four feet high. It is planted every year and dies in the autumn when the frost comes. This, however, is not the cotton plant in its native state. In India and Peru, both of which are tropical countries, it grew, and still grows, wild in the form of a tree. The native cotton plant does not die down each autumn but lives on through the decades as might an apple tree. The cotton tree is, in fact, about as big as a peach tree cut cone-like in shape. In the Andes of South America it is no uncommon thing to find a cotton tree growing wild in the autumn woods and presenting a white mass of cotton in the boll.

COTTON BOLLS

When Europeans first went to India, they were much

impressed with the cotton which they found the natives using. They had long used wool and they called this plant fiber *tree wool.* Cotton weaving and printing was even then highly developed in India. The use of this cotton cloth spread west. The Moors brought cotton to Spain in the ninth century. The crusaders learned something of the cloth made of it when they went on their pilgrimages. Its use by no means became general, however, until much later. When the Portuguese ships sailed around Africa and traded with India in the sixteenth century, they began to bring back cotton cloth in quantities. But in the time of Elizabeth, even up to our Revolutionary War, cotton cloth was little used by Westerners. The ships of England were at that time going all about the world as forerunners of that trade that was later to make her great. At home she was learning how to spin cotton and was laying a foundation for her future leadership as a cloth-making nation. The industry was held back, however, by the shortage of raw cotton. England got all of it that she could from the East. She had found native Americans growing cotton in the West Indies and as far south as Brazil, and bought what she could from them. Cotton, it seemed, was produced nearly everywhere in America except in what is now the United States. Later it came to pass that one-fourth of the United States produced more than half of the cotton in the world. When white men first came, however, no cotton plants were growing in that particular part of the New World. Cotton is not a natural growth in the region that has since come to be known as the "Land of Cotton."

COTTON PLANTS ON THE MISSISSIPPI DELTA

Before the Revolutionary War, cotton was quite generally grown in America, even as far north as Pennsylvania, but was little used except by the housewife in spinning cloth for clothes for her own family. All this time the detail that was holding back the development of the use of cotton was the difficulty in separating the lint from the seed. The seeds were picked out tediously by hand, and the family that separated four pounds of cotton in a week was doing well. Thus it would take about two years for a family to produce a bale of cotton. Up to 1784 the report of cotton was so low that when, in that year, eight bales were sent to England it was seized by the government on suspicion because it was not believed that America could produce so much of the staple. Then, in 1793, Eli Whitney invented the cotton gin which was the greatest event of all the ages of cotton history. Cotton production in America increased by unbelievable quantities. Cotton planting through the South became the most popular sort of farming. The planters became wealthy and increased their holdings. The southern states of America seized world leadership in cotton production and have held it from that day to this. With the development of its cheap manufacture by machinery the whole world has tended toward the use of cotton as clothing, and it now covers more backs than any other staple. Of the fiber plants of the world, this tropical tree has become the undisputed master. Whole communities, like New England, have grown rich from setting up cotton mills. Cotton is a crop of commerce. It is not consumed but shipped all around the world. It is the greatest crop for commerce that there is. None other brings so much outside money to the United States. None other so vitally affects the trade of the world. No other brings so much employment, so much comfort, to members of the human race.

It is a strange position that this tropical plant, this member of the mallow family, occupies in the United States. It did not grow here naturally. It was a foreigner that was brought in from elsewhere but found that America was a better place for it than any other

CONTOURED FIELDS OF COTTON IN MISSISSIPPI

in which it had been planted. In its transplanting, it was brought to live a life that was far different from that which it had known in its native tropics. It became the creature of a single summer rather than a tree that lived through the years. Yet it thrived by this artificial life and its glory steadily grew.

The cotton plant in nature grows through the years as does a peach tree. In the United States, which is not tropical, it cannot live this sort of life because it cannot endure frost. It must be planted in the spring and brought to flower and fruit before frost comes in the autumn. Then it will blight and die and a new crop of it must be planted the next spring. It has become a field crop that must be newly planted every year, where once it was a tree that lived long in the woods.

Some years ago, when American scientific cotton growers began farming in Hawaii, they planted cotton. It prospered and bore crops but did not die in the autumn. The cotton plants lived through the frostless winters of that region and again bore a crop the next year. They grew larger with the passing seasons until they became trees. The crops they bore were excellent in quality and quantity. Some of these trees grew to be four or five years old and still produced heavily. These island cotton growers began to figure the amount of their yield and whether more cotton could be harvested by growing it on trees in an orchard or on plants that died every year in the field. It began to look as if orchard cotton were the better idea. In fact, it might have proved to be the better way had not an unforeseen event happened. The cotton trees were attacked by certain insects that destroyed the crop. The farmers were not able to get rid of the insects. They were forced to abandon their cotton orchards. All this does not prove that a time may not come when cotton orchards may be grown in the tropics and cotton farming go back to the basis on which Nature first produced it. But for the present this tropical plant, grown in an unnatural way in a temperate zone, yields best returns of vegetable wool for man's use.

CHAPTER XIX

THE CACTUS FAMILY

IT IS a strange thing that one of the wettest families of plants in all the world should find its favorite home on the deserts of Arizona and Mexico.

Members of the cactus family stand out in the midst of the great dry spaces year after year and, despite the lack of moisture all about them, are found to be not unlike water-soaked sponges if one but cuts into them. Men who are famishing on the desert for lack of water often keep themselves alive by cutting into cacti, squeezing water out of the spongy flesh, and drinking it. Rabbits and desert rats sometimes dig holes in them, eat their moist pulp, and save themselves from death from thirst.

These desert plants have a way of storing water when it rains and taking the greatest care of it that it may last them for months or even years. It is only by doing so that they are able to keep alive in an arid country. Plants in other regions need not look so far ahead because it rains every few weeks and there is always moisture in the ground. Whenever they want a drink, they have only to draw it up through their roots. But where there is no moisture in the ground for great stretches of time, some other method must be developed for keeping a store of it.

The giant cactus of Arizona, whose proper and formal

SAHUARO CACTI GROWING IN ARIZONA

name is the *sahuaro*, grows out in the desert, often in one straight column thirty or forty feet high. It is a tree, but one of the strangest trees in the world. It is a tree without a single branch. It is a tree without leaves. It is a tree with fluted sides like the pillar of a Greek temple. The pleats in its sides can expand or contract so that it may be a foot bigger around after it has had a drink than before. It is a tree that is covered with prickly spines from tip to toe. Neither man nor beast is likely to lean up against it more than once. It is a tree with soft flesh built around a framework of ribs. These ribs are used by the Indians in building their huts but the flesh of the cactus will never hold together so that it may be cut up into lumber. It is, in fact, built upon a dozen ideas that are entirely different from those back of the form of other trees.

All these peculiar traits of the sahuaro grow out of the fact that it lives in the desert and must store up water for the time when there will be no rain and the ground will be dry.

The sahuaro has no leaves. Everybody knows that it takes much water to keep leaves going. They are filled with water. Shut off their water supply for an hour and they begin to wilt. An oak tree gives out barrels of water every day through its leaves. If a sahuaro had to furnish moisture for a leafy top, it would be pumped dry and die in three days. To live in the desert, members of the cactus family long ago had to do away with leaves.

But the food for most plants is manufactured by their leaves. It is the green in the leaves that performs some miracle with sunbeams to make it possible for them to take carbon dioxide out of the air, combine it with water, and make sugar for plant food. The sahuaro, having no leaves, developed a green skin that would make sugar. All the cacti have green skins that do the work of leaves.

This green skin of the cacti is smooth as leather and water-tight. These plants are sealed and varnished on the outside so that none of the water within can escape. If the dry air of the desert could get at their moisture, it would sap it up in a short time.

Inside there are ribs or slats running lengthwise of the plant and giving it form. Thus it becomes a green, thorn-studded bag stretched loosely over these slats, as the covering of a dirigible is stretched over its framework. In the bag is a spongy filling of no great degree of firmness. When there are rains, the roots suck up the water and fill the inside of the plant. The pleats of the outer skin fill out. The cactus fairly struts with its fullness. The inside is nearly as wet as is that of a watermelon.

Then the dry weather comes. The moisture sealed up in the plant is held there and used very economically for such purposes as growth and flowering. Thus it becomes possible that the cactus should break into bloom on the desert while all else is parched and seared.

These blooms appear in dense circles at the very top of the giant cactus. They begin as green buds as big as figs. Then they open into big, white, yellow-hearted flowers, high set on these massive water towers of the desert. The flowers again give way to an oval, crimson fruit, datelike in shape but as big as a peach. The Papago Indians that live in the cactus country are very fond of this fruit. To be sure, it is not easy to get at, on the top of the sahuaro with its multitude of thorns that make climbing impossible. But the Indian women can reach the tops with the ribs of dead sahuaros and knock the fruit down. They return from the plains with baskets full of fruit which they convert into preserves for later use.

These giant cacti are thought to live to be three or four hundred years old. They grow mostly in single columns, but occasionally, probably because of some injury to the crest, they branch out. Side arms, sometimes to the number of six or eight, put forth and then turn upward. Thus does the great plant take on the form of candlesticks with many branches.

The giant may stand on the plain surrounded by neighborly greasewoods, catclaws, mesquites, sagebrush, and chollas. Its presence may be taken as an invitation to the woodpecker which penetrates even into these solitudes, and a single column may become the home of a dozen such. They can squeeze in between the thorns, and excavate their homes in the soft pulp. The sahuaro, that it may waste little of its moisture, immediately surrounds the wound made by the woodpecker with fiber and plasters it over, thus making a cool and waterproofed pocket for the woodpecker. There a woodpecker family may grow up one year and the next the same apartment may be occupied by a pigmy owl. The sahuaro thus becomes a tower-like apartment house of the desert.

There are barrel cacti on the desert of a similar breed, but fatter than the giant and rarely growing more than four or five feet tall. There are varieties of the same general make-up that grow in clusters but never more than a foot tall. Then there are the cholla and the prickly pear, that are members of the cactus family, a little further removed but close kin to each other, as they have the same general growing scheme. They are like each other in that they develop joint by joint. Most people know the prickly pear, which is the most widespread of all the cacti. Its plant is made up of one flat lobe linked to another. Thus it may become a sprawling

PRICKLY PEAR IN BLOOM

bush as high as a man's head. Its flat lobes are fleshy, green, air-tight, and, in accord with the habit of cacti, stored full of moisture. It protects itself against drought on the same principle as that used by the sahuaro.

The cholla is built of joints linked together as are those of the prickly pear. Instead of being flat, however, they are round. They go to a much greater extreme than the prickly pear in the use of thorns. They become, in fact, thorn balls with needles sticking out in all directions.

Few objects in this world are more forbidding than the cholla bush, standing at the edge of the dry lands with a million daggers in place and ready to impale whatever living thing approaches it.

The tricks that members of the vegetable world play to get themselves planted in new places are without end. Few of them, however, resort to more extreme methods than the cholla. What they try to do is to force themselves on some member of the animal world, to attach their joints to their victim, there to stick for a while and be dropped at a place some distance away. These barbed joints of the cholla break off very easily from the mother plant. If, therefore, an animal should as much as brush against one of these plants, the needle points will enter the skin and stick. The ball to which they are attached will then break off from the mother plant. The animal will walk away with a needle stuck in its skin and a joint of the cholla plant attached to the needle. It may ride for days on this animal before it is rubbed off. When it does come off, however, it will try to take root and establish a new cholla colony.

The prickly pear is the best known and most widely spread of the cacti. It, like the rest of the family, is a native American, and is primarily a child of the desert. This cactus cousin, however, is given to ranging into the haunts of other plant growth. It is found from Colorado to Chile in its native state. Since white men came to America, it has been taken to Spain, Italy, Africa, and Australia, and has made new homes for itself in those lands. In some of them it has become a weed and must be fought as an injurious introduction. In South

Europe and Africa its fruit, known as the Indian fig, is more highly prized than in its native haunts. This fruit is much like that which grows on top of the giant cactus and is put to similar uses.

The United States Government has given much study

THE THORNY CHOLLA OF THE CACTUS FAMILY

to the possibility of converting the prickly pear into a useful plant. It has found, for instance, that it grows freely in the semi-desert cattle country of the Southwest when there are seasons of drought that produce none of the grasses upon which live stock usually depend. Its fat joints are good cattle feed. The cattle would like to eat it, but the thorns with which it is covered make this impossible. Cattle starve to death when vast stores of good food is only a thorn's length out of their reach. How, the government has been asking, can this prickly pear, that grows when other plants are dying from drought, be used for the purpose of feeding live stock?

The prickly pear has two kinds of thorns—long, bristly ones and tiny, fuzzy ones. Either is painful to the mouth of the hungry cow that attacks this plant. Some prickly pears are thickly covered with these thorns and some are almost thornless. Cattle can eat the spineless ones. In the cattle country, however, these are likely to be so closely grazed that they die out. But those with many thorns grow and prosper.

Government experts have tried cultivating the prickly pear. Joints of the plants may be spaced along a furrow and dirt plowed over them. They will take root and grow. With the ground thus loosened for their roots and broken to admit more moisture when it rains, they grow much bigger than in the wild state. It was found, in fact, that cultivated prickly pears produce stupendous crops. At San Antonio, Texas, fifty tons of them were grown to the acre. Brownsville did even better. It produced 105 tons of prickly pear to the acre. That, of course, was a great deal of cattle feed if a way could be found to use it.

Someone in Texas thought of a novel scheme for feeding prickly pears to starving cattle. Blowtorches were taken into the fields where they grew and the thorns were singed off the plants as they stood. The cattle then fell upon the plants and devoured them. They ate only as far as the singeing had gone and stopped. One could feed his cattle only as many prickly pears as he wanted them to have by limiting his singeing. He could go out day after day and feed his cattle, not by hauling hay out to them, but by burning the thorns off his cactus plants.

The crop could stand out in the field until it was

NATURE'S PINCUSHION

wanted, keeping green and tasty. It did not have to be harvested, stored, or cared for. It did not even need be fenced in. Its thorns were its protection. It could stand unfenced in the field or on the open range in perfect safety. The hired man with a blowtorch could go out to feed the stock as it became necessary. Having been eaten down, the plants would start again and grow another crop of thorny joints that in their turn could not be eaten until the flame was applied.

Southward through Mexico there are endless varieties of cacti. Generally speaking, they are children of the desert. Plants in the beginning came out of the water. There were water plants before there were land plants. Land plants developed from water plants that were scattered along the shore. With their feet in the water and their heads

CACTI CAN BE ARRANGED IN FORMAL DESIGNS FOR GARDENS

in the air, they prospered and gathered strength. As the centuries passed, they marched farther and farther inland. They became able to live with less and less water.

Yet most plants still like moist places. The densest growth is where the ground is wet. As it grows drier and drier, plants tend to disappear. They struggle out on to the plains where the battle for life is hard because of a shortage of water. Finally, the plain becomes a desert. Here for millions of years plants have tried to establish themselves. The members of the cactus family have come nearer doing so than any other. They have overcome the difficulties of the desert by storing water within themselves and then sealing it in, so that it may not be evaporated. Of all the plants of this world, coming in the beginning as they did out of the water, the cacti have made the longest march away from it. They are the most advanced plant outriders into the desert stretches that the world knows.

But there are members of the cactus family that are not desert plants. In that stretch of territory that extends from the United States to the land of fire which is at the end of South America, there is much desert that is not far removed from marshy stretches. The cacti, after having developed peculiarities fitting them for life in the arid regions, have often wandered back into the jungle, and there have grown into strange forms and associations.

There is, for instance, the night-blooming cereus. It has become a climbing plant, a sort of vine that strings itself among the branches of trees like a strange-jointed hose. There, upon occasion, it breaks into midnight bloom, into glorious white flowers, sometimes a foot across. It is cultivated in many a garden or conservatory, where it is a matter of interest and curiosity. But it is a thorned, fluted cactus with strange habits that has got away from its natural family ties and is disporting itself in circles that are not those of most of its cousins.

Chapter XX

THE BANANA FAMILY

ABRAHAM LINCOLN probably never saw a banana. Charles Dickens, who died in 1870, is not likely to have ever had an opportunity to buy one on the streets of his London. Henry Wadsworth Longfellow, settling down to a quiet life in Cambridge, Massachusetts, after publishing *Tales of a Wayside Inn* in the eighteen sixties, was nearer to bananas than most men of his generation. If he had gone down to the Boston docks on a certain day in the year 1870, he might have seen a Captain Baker unloading from his schooner the first cargo of bananas that ever came to that port.

Bananas were almost unknown in the United States, or in Europe, or anywhere outside of the tropics, fifty years ago. They were not generally known up to the end of the last century. People of the present generation, having seen a bunch of bananas hanging on a hook any day in the year in any fruit store they may have entered, may have supposed that bananas always had been for sale. But the banana is a new fruit to people in temperate zone countries.

Bananas do not grow very close to New York or St. Louis or Dallas, Texas. Their home is in the tropics. They are at their best in Central America. They have to be shipped long distances by water and rail. They have to be handled very carefully or they will spoil before they reach the market. Fifty years ago there were few fast ships and there was little cold storage. Nobody had thought of its being possible so to handle the fruit of this broad-leaved shrub of the tropics that it could be offered for sale to all the world. Putting a bunch of bananas on the hook in the fruit stores of Paducah, Kentucky, and Carson City, Nevada, is almost as new a thing as parking an automobile near the curb outside those stores.

While new as a food in the temperate zones, the banana is among the oldest of cultivated plants. When Alexander the Great invaded India, more than 2,000 years ago, he found large plantations given over to bananas. Their cultivation is equally old in Africa. Whether they were grown by the Aztecs and the Incas in America before Europeans came, is a question that has never been settled. Most students of banana history now hold that the banana was not known in the Western Hemisphere until after Columbus' discovery. They believe that it was brought to the West Indies by the Spaniards and that it spread rapidly all over the American tropics until this region became the greatest of all producers of this fruit.

A great many people believe that bananas are harvested from trees that grow wild in Central America and elsewhere. It is true that the banana plant grows wild there. Banana fruit, however, is never harvested from wild plants. The plant has to be cared for in just the right way or it will not bear fruit. It seldom or never finds the proper conditions in the wild state.

WORKER WITH MACHETE HARVESTS BANANAS

No fruit from wild bananas ever reaches the outside market.

The banana plant is one of the strangest in the vegetable kingdom.

There are few other plants so closely related to it that they are put in the same family. It has one relative that is fairly well known in northern countries. This is the great purple canna that grows as an ornamental plant in gardens and parks. It is a member of the banana family, and its stalk and leaves grow much as do those of its fruit-bearing cousin.

The members of the banana family are like the palms and the grasses in that they are inside growers rather than plants that put on layers of growth on the outside, as do forest trees. The new leaves that add to the size of the plant grow from the inside. The bananas are different from the grasses or the palms, however, in the peculiar way in which they form their stems.

The palm builds itself an outer shell-like trunk which is hollow and never becomes any bigger around. It grows out of the top of this trunk. Members of the grass family, such as corn, grow from the inside but build up jointed stalks for themselves. The banana plant has neither an outside trunk nor a stalk. The body that it builds up, sometimes forty feet in height, is made of nothing more than the sheaths of the leaves which it produces. It puts one of these inside another, as one paper funnel might be put inside another, until it has built its trunk.

Through the center of this trunk a channel has been kept open. Up through this, when the time is right, the flower stalk forces itself. If the banana plants grow wild and are forced together in a jungle, they are only small plants like those in the canna patch. If, however, they have been planted at proper distances in rich fields and the weeds kept from robbing them of sun or plant food, they may grow to be fifteen or twenty feet high and six inches through the trunk. Under exceptional conditions, banana trees sometimes grow to be forty feet high and two feet thick. There is no other large plant which is not supported by a woody stem.

Not many plants are always ready to give a demonstration of how they grow, as is the banana. A vigorous young plant six feet tall may be used in an experiment. It may be cut off smoothly two feet above the ground at ten o'clock in the morning. Almost immediately it will begin to push up a button at its center. By six o'clock the same afternoon it will have run up a stalk of tightly wound leaves two feet high. In another day it will have flung to the breeze a crown of leaves four feet above the cut.

The banana plant spreads out a cluster of great leaves at the top. Sometimes these leaves are ten feet long and two feet wide. With them the plant, which is likely to be about ten months old by the time the leaves are produced, has completed its growth except for the fruiting

It is now that the great bud comes crowding up through the channel that has been kept open for it. When it first appears at the crown, it is as big as an ear of corn and does not look unlike one. It keeps on growing. It is so heavy that it soon bends its stem over until it hangs downward. After a bit the husks fall off and the little green bananas appear with their tips pointing straight to the side. Later they turn their tips upward. In three or four months these little bananas have grown into the bunches of commerce.

If left alone, this banana tree, after bearing this one bunch of fruit on its central stalk, will die. In practice it is sure to be visited by two skilful workmen on the plantation, whose business it is to do so when bananas are ready for the picking. One of these is called the *cutter* and the other is called the *backer*. The cutter has a long stick with a knife at the end of it. He selects a point several feet from the top of the plant and cuts the trunk of the tree in such a way as to weaken it but not to break it. Thus weakened, it lets the bunch of bananas down slowly and without a crash. The backer receives it on his shoulder. The cutter severs the stem, above and below the fruit, with his machete. The backer carries it away to the nearest pack mule or tramcar, and it is on its way to market. The cutter chops the tree off at the ground and leaves it to decay and return to the soil.

Bananas are something like sugar cane in manner of growth. When the grown plant is cut down, young ones spring up from the old root. A field, once planted, will go on growing for five, ten, fifteen, sometimes twenty, years. To grow properly and bear good fruit, however, it must be given a great deal of care.

The root of the banana plant, called the head, is something like a great bulb. It has "eyes" not unlike those of a potato. New sprouts come out from the sides of it. Fields of bananas are planted by cutting these sprouts off old heads and putting them in the proper rows. The heads themselves may be cut up and planted as are potatoes. Care must be taken that each piece has an eye. Soon the new plants begin to produce sprouts or suckers. If these plants were allowed to have their own way, they soon would be growing so close together that they could not thrive and would bear no fruit. This is what they do in the wild state. But by trimming out the suckers, the people who cultivate bananas can keep just the right number of them growing and young ones coming on all the time to take the places of those that

CAREFUL HARVESTING OF BANANAS PREVENTS BRUISING

ripen, bear fruit, and are cut down. In this way, field bananas are ripening every day in the year. There is really no special time of year when bananas are in season. They are ripening all the time.

Most plants grow fruit for a very particular reason. They want to get their seeds planted and the fruit helps them to that end. This is not true of the banana. There are no seeds in its fruit that will grow if they are planted. Banana plants cannot be grown from the fruit. All of which runs counter to the common law of the vegetable kingdom.

As a matter of fact, there are the remnants of seeds in the banana. Tiny specks that doubtless were once seeds may be seen near its center. There was surely a time when the banana plant produced seeds in its fruit that would grow. Then it learned to send up young plants from its roots. New potato plants, it will be remembered, are now produced almost altogether from the "eyes" on the tubers that grow under the ground. Some potato plants rarely bloom now. They do not need to do so to carry on their race. Neither does the banana. It does not need to produce seed and so has lost the ability to do so. But man has found that, by creating favorable conditions, he can induce the banana plant to grow its fruit as of old. He has, in fact, coaxed this plant through the centuries to improve the quality of its fruit. But that fruit has lost the vital quality that would enable it to carry the spark of life on to another generation.

Besides Asia, Africa, the Canary Islands, and tropical America, bananas grow abundantly in the Philippines, Hawaii, the Malays, Fiji, and generally through the South Seas. It was Central America, however, that offered the best of all opportunities for their cultivation on a large scale. All along its eastern coast were rich lands visited by heavy rainfall and covered with dense jungles. Many of these jungles, during the past generation, have been converted into rich and productive plantations.

The manner in which this is done is most interesting.

The underbrush is cut down, the land staked off, and a banana "eye" is planted every twenty feet or so. Then the forest itself is cut down. The heavy timber forms a complete layer of brush over the land. This is left on the ground and the banana plants come up through it. In this hot country of much rainfall, the tangled mass quickly decays and goes back into the soil, enriching it. Five or six stalks grow up from every banana plant root and a great area becomes a sea of waving broad leaves.

Light tramways are run through the banana field every few hundred yards. When the trees come into bearing, the bunches are carried to these tramways. They in turn feed railways which carry the fruit down to the coast. There it is met by specially built banana steamships that arrive on regular schedules. One of these ships will hold 50,000 to 75,000 bunches of bananas. The industry has developed in such a way that steamships, sailing from New York, talk by radio to the plantations, and these cut and hurry the fruit to the coast. There it is received still fresh and green, hung in the ship, and kept under the conditions that are best for its proper ripening. Hurried North, the fruit is taken from the ships, placed in refrigerator cars, and shipped by rail to every point in the nation. It is sold every day in the year in every village from coast to coast. The whole journey from the plantation in Central America to the lunch basket of the boy in Topeka, Kansas, must be made before this fruit-child of the tropics decays.

The arrangement of the bananas on the bunch is interesting. They appear in clusters which are called *hands*. The bananas themselves play the part of fingers on these hands. There may be from ten to twenty-five bananas on a hand. A bunch of bananas which has six of these clusters is called a *six-hand* bunch. If it has less than six hands, it is not good enough to send to market. A typical bunch, such as is seen in the fruit store, is likely to have about nine hands and 150 bananas. Bunches have been harvested with as many as twenty-two hands and 300 bananas.

THE FLOWER BUDS OUT AT THE TOP OF THE STALK

Bananas are always green when harvested. Most fruit is better when it stays on the tree and is picked when ripe. This is not true of bananas. They are flat and tasteless when they ripen on the tree. Natives of the tropic islands cut the bananas when green and ripen them off the tree when they want fruit for their own use.

This fact about bananas is very fortunate since it helps so much in marketing them. The bunches when green will stand a good deal of knocking around without injury. They will last long enough before getting ripe and soft to make the long trip to market. If it were necessary to let them hang on the trees until they were ripe, it would never be possible to distribute them widely.

The bananas that are most often seen in market are known as Great Michaels, sometimes spoken of as "Big Mikes." As these bananas ripen, they turn from green to yellow. There is also a variety of red bananas. These latter are stubbier, thicker bananas of good quality. The public, however, has formed the habit of buying yellow bananas and the market demands them. Other varieties of smaller bananas are popular where grown.

Then there is the plantain which is not quite like a banana. It does not ripen into sweetness. The starch in it does not turn to sugar as it does in the banana. To be eaten, it must be cooked. It is an important food to millions of people living in the tropics but is not shipped out. As a food its place is something like that of the potato.

It is difficult to tell a plantain tree from a banana tree. When the bud comes out at the top, it turns down just as does the banana. When the fruit appears on the bunch, however, instead of turning its tips up as does the banana, it turns them down.

In many tropical countries the plantain is more important to the natives than is the banana. In Santo Domingo, for example, it is the main item of food for thousands of people. Fried or baked, it is delicious. Its meat is firmer than that of the banana and tastes quite different. It is bigger and lends itself better to being cooked. The natives eat it boiled but in this form it is not very palatable to the man from the North. Roasted in the ashes, however, it becomes a food fit for a king. Where it grows wild and hangs on the tree at all seasons of the year, the natives have few food problems.

Many people who often eat bananas have failed to learn how to tell when they are at their best. Bananas that are bright yellow with a possible tinge of green left in them are not yet at their best. They may be eaten, but they are not so good as they will be when they are riper. The starch in them has only partly turned to sugar. Keep them a few days and they will be much improved. Their yellow color will then be deeper. Presently black splotches will begin to appear in their skins. They are now getting truly ripe. They will be better when the skin has become quite black. From the time when they begin to show black splotches, however, they are ready for eating. Their food value is high. They are good for growing children. Nature has put them up in germ-proof and dirt-proof packages. Science has developed few envelopes that take such good care of their contents and are so easy to open.

Chapter XXI

THE PINE FAMILY

THE PINE family is one of the oldest in the plant world. Geologists have their own ways of telling which of the layers of rocks that make up the earth's crust are the oldest. Generally, the one that is on the bottom was laid down first. Many of these rocks bear the impressions of the vegetation that was about when they were being formed. A layer of white sand, for example, might be washed down from the mountains. Autumn winds might cover this sand with maple leaves. Then a rainstorm on a red hillside might bring down a deposit of red earth and put it on top of the white sand. Both layers might turn to stone. Ten million years later some geologist might dig into this stone and find the impressions of maple leaves. He would know that maple trees had been growing before the stone was formed.

It is in this way that it has become known that club mosses were among the early plants to develop. It is in this way also that cat-tails that grow in the marshes are found to be of a family that runs far back into the past. It is found out that trees of the pine family grew and thrived long before those that have broad leaves existed anywhere in the world. They are an older order of tree.

The kangaroo is a survival of an old order of animals and is less highly developed than such active specimens as the cat. The pine, by the same token, is far behind other families of trees in certain respects. Its leaves are not at all complicated. It has a very simple form of seed germ which compares poorly with the elaborate flowers of many trees. This germ stands out naked and unprotected. It is because of this that scientists call the members of this family *gymnosperms,* which means "naked seeds."

There is little difficulty in telling the members of the pine family because, in a way, they look alike and are quite different in appearance from other trees. The cedar, the hemlock, the yew tree, the fir, the spruce, the larch, the juniper, the cypress, are all relatives, as may be easily seen. One would think that it would be easy to find a handier name than *gymnosperms* for them. He might think of calling them cone-bearing trees, but this idea would be spoiled when it was found that the red cedar and other true junipers bear berries instead of cones. He might call them needle-leaved trees, but the scales of the cedar would hardly fit that description. He might call them evergreens, but the cypress and larches shed their leaves, and the magnolia, which is outside the family, is an evergreen. This "naked seed" name of the scientists seems to be about the only one that will fit.

The pine tree family came into the world before there were insects to carry pollen from one flower to another as is done for the younger families. They do not depend on insects. Instead they shake out dense clouds of yellow pollen that fills the air, floats on streams, and often drifts in yellow masses along the shore. This pollen while floating in the air reaches the naked ovules that are to become seeds and fertilizes them.

The pine family is a very hardy group. Its members are likely to be found growing far up to the north. They fringe many a jagged coast and break the boisterous winds that romp in from the sea. They climb high up mountain sides and thrive above the line which other timber cannot cross. They are children of the snows, defying the winds.

As one goes up a lofty mountain, it is as if he were traveling north toward the pole. He passes through belts where the climate is successively like that of Michigan, of Manitoba, of Hudson Bay, of the Arctic itself. The broad-leaved trees disappear and only the pine relatives are to be found. The upper wooded levels of high mountains are dark with fir, spruce, or pine. The mountain may rise so high that finally there is reached a point where the hardiest of all trees fights for a mere existence. The last of these, the final survivor, the furthest outrider of the tree world, is likely to be a gnarled and ancient limber pine. It grows at timber line under the severest conditions that a tree can face and still keep alive. These timber line pines appear to be old beyond reckoning. They are bent, knotted, tortured, as if from a lifetime on the rack. A few straggling arms, green-tipped, reach out helter-skelter, but keep enough leaves in the sun to provide food for a meager growth. But they are the hardiest of all trees that live, for they grow where it is higher and colder than any other tree can endure.

The fact that they live among the snows has had a great deal to do with the nature of the members of the pine family. Their needle leaves are especially constructed so that the winds cannot get hold of them, and for the shedding of snow. Snowflakes slide off their

THE PINE TREE THAT GROWS HIGHEST UP THE MOUNTAIN SIDE

polished surfaces, sift between their narrow shafts. The broad-leaved trees, if it were not for the fact that they shed their foliage in autumn, would doubtless be broken down by the snow in regions where the fall is heavy.

Then there is the structure of the pine tree or the spruce or the fir. There is the tall central bole reaching high. The branches are short, gnarled, and twisted.

The wood of which they are made will bend far before it will break. The severest of winters would have difficulty in piling enough snow on one of these branches to snap it. A tree as straight as a lance may reach high into the air with only such short limbs as to make it appear that it was a flagpole decorated in greens for a celebration. Or another tree may take the shape of a cone coming to a tip at the top. There are no long branches high up to bear the weight of snow nor to give the winds a heavy pull nor otherwise to cause trouble when winter storms grow rough. These trees are built in this way so that they may resist wind and snow.

It was because their boughs were limber that man, as he developed through his earlier stages, depended on these trees for the bows that for centuries flung the arrows of war. It was because their trunks were tall and straight and strong that the pine was known as the "sailor's tree" through the centuries when ships crossed the seas under canvas. It is because they produce great straight logs that are handy at the sawmill and smooth, easily worked boards that lend themselves to the purposes of him who would build a house or fashion the toy of a child, that they have held first place among lumber-producing trees through the centuries.

The cone in which most of the pine relatives put up their seeds is a novelty in the vegetable world. It begins as a mere backbone to which are attached the seed germs, each one covered by a scale that is just taking form. The scale leaves the seed germ exposed until the pollen to fertilize it has drifted in. Then it clamps down and shields the seed from harm while it is developing. The cone begins to take form. It becomes a woody structure one fourth of an inch long in the case of the white cedar and fourteen inches long with the sugar pine, from tip to tip.

CONES AND NEEDLES OF THE EASTERN WHITE PINE

There are usually seeds at the base of every scale. These scales are likely to be held down with resin while the seeds are developing. When they are ripe, the resin and the cone dry out and the scales lift themselves from over the seeds and give them a chance to escape. Each little seed is provided with a wing that, caught by a stiff wind, may carry it far. These trees which, through the ages, have fought an unceasing battle with wind and snow, here make use of one of their ancient enemies to serve one of their most important ends, that of broadcasting their seeds.

The seeds hidden in these cones are attractive food for certain birds and particularly for squirrels. The cone is a very good protector, but the wise tree squirrel knows when the cone is ripe so that it may pull off one scale after another with its handlike paws and feast on these seeds. It knows, too, when it should cut down the cones for its winter store and carefully hide them away.

The cones, which the squirrel cut down and carried to its nest, the seeds which it devoured through the long winter, were a clear loss to the forest. At times, however, this tree dweller buried pine cones in the ground as it does hickory nuts, and these, if it did not come back to dig them up would have a good chance to start young trees. And now, since man has come into the forests to select the seeds of the best of the pine varieties for planting, the squirrel has turned out to be a great help. The easiest way to get pine cones properly equipped with seed, man finds, is to rob the squirrel's nest. The stores of cones gathered by these little animals have furnished seeds for replanting the forests of France and many a western mountain side that has been swept by fire.

The cedar tree develops a berry instead of a cone. It uses a more modern method of getting its seeds distributed than does the pine. It ripens its berries in the autumn and hangs them out for the winter when other food for birds is likely to be scarce. It paints them a brilliant blue that they may be easy to see. The birds carry them up and down fence rows and drop them. This is the reason that one is so likely to see cedars growing along old fences in so many parts of the country.

The system of the yew tree is a little different. It develops a cup in which it places its seeds. As autumn comes on, this cup grows scarlet and meaty, and the birds find it good to eat. The yew, however, poisons the seed that it places inside the cup. The birds know that it is poison and so refuse to swallow it. They eat the cup and throw away the seed. Thus the yew succeeds in getting its seed carried about and planted by the birds.

These dense evergreen trees are of great importance to the winter birds. There are certain of these that elect to stay in the North through the months of cold, and these sorely need protection from the bitter winds, from snow and sleet. They find it far in the bosoms of somber cedars and pines.

There is the sturdy chickadee, tiny scrap of valor, that manages to keep cheerful in all sorts of weather. There is the junco and the noisy tufted titmouse and the white crested nuthatches that hang head downward on branches and trunks of trees while they hunt for insect eggs. The ruby-crowned kinglet comes down from the far north woods and, although never having seen a human being, is not at all shy of man.

To be sure, these winter birds are wrapped in thick layers of downy feathers that form the best of overcoats, but even at that who would want to sit out on a bare twig of the spreading elm when a northern winter is on? They establish their homes in the hearts of doughty evergreens and there defy the cold. They come out from time to time for food, of which they consume a surprising amount, considering the fact that under their feathers they may be no larger than the last joint of a man's thumb. But the stoves burn brightly inside the winter birds. They keep a temperature of 106, which, for a human being, would be a raging fever, and in doing so, burn much fuel. They eat many weed seeds and thus render great service to man. The tassel of many a weed is lifted above the snow and there carries the seeds that will mingle with next summer's crops and make much cultivation necessary. The snow is frozen into a hard crust, and thus forms the dinner table for the winter birds. They visit the dry weed tops, shake out the seeds which fall on the white crust of snow, hop down and devour them. Also they climb about the trunks and limbs of trees and there find that the insects of last summer have left their eggs in the cracks of the bark for next year's hatching. By picking these out, they have their eggs for breakfast and nip the summer's insect crop in the bud.

Many are the members of this family of trees that have served man through the cycling years. It is doubtless true that more houses have been built in the United States of white pine lumber than of anything else. The white pine, with branches that go straight out and with slender needles arranged in clusters of five, was, from the beginning, the favorite lumber tree of the North. Unfortunately, lumbermen have cut down most of the original forests and have failed to plant or provide for young trees to replace them. Then, of late, a mighty blight, the white pine blister rust, has crossed the ocean and attacked this great tree and threatens to do it to death. It presents one of the great tragedies of the vegetable world, a case where one outlaw tribe of plants may ruthlessly and seemingly without purpose fall upon and destroy another. In this case it is a tiny spore riding on the wind, a member of the mushroom family described in the chapter which treated that group, that is the messenger of death.

In many ways the long-leaf pine of the South, extending from Virginia to Texas, is to that region what the white pine is to the North. Its strangest feature is the unbelievably long needles that it grows. These strange leaves sometimes develop to a length of eighteen inches and hang like the stringy locks of a witch from the tips of its branches. The long-leaf pine, too, is the center of an unusual industry which is based almost entirely upon it. It yields every year 700,000,000 pounds of rosin, used in the manufacture of soap, wax, and varnishes, and 25,000,000 gallons of turpentine, largely used in paints. Thus is it the basis of a great industry, the existence of which is little appreciated, an industry built on the fact that pine is resinous, has within it a gummy substance which oozes out in great teardrops whenever the tree is wounded. In the South the trees are deliberately wounded that this resin may appear and be harvested. The raw material is called resin or gum turpentine which, when refined, becomes turpentine and rosin. The pine trees that grew ages ago laid down quantities of this rosin. It is found in a fossil form which is known as amber.

Spruce trees, silver-tipped and long-coned, are among the noble sentinels of the north woods. Some of them sweep across the American continent from Nova Scotia to Alaska. They furnish the wood pulp from which is

BLUE SPRUCES

made nearly all the paper upon which the newspapers of the world are printed. They provide noble timbers for shipbuilding and soft wood for the carving of toys.

Their cone-shaped forms and attractive foliage make them the most widely used evergreens in American gardens. They often stand in dense forests where every tree is from two hundred to three hundred years old and straight as a spar. Sound trees have often been cut and, when the rings of cross sections of their trunks were counted, have been found to be four hundred years old. The United States Forest Service describes such a tree that was cut at Pittsfield, Vermont, which was three hundred twenty years old, had a diameter of thirty-six inches fourteen feet from the ground, and five inches at a height of one hundred twenty feet.

Such trees are not unusually old as matters go in the forests. There are many rugged pine trees standing in the western mountains that, when felled and their structure examined, would be found to be 1,000 years old. Every living tree puts on a new layer of growth each year as it might a cloak. This layer of growth covers its every part, from the tips of its roots to the tips of its outmost branch. It forms a ring on its trunk outside that of the year before. When the tree is cut down, the rings may be counted on the stump, and each stands for a year of age. A thousand of them would mean that the tree is 1,000 years old.

But an examination of the body of the tree may reveal much more than this. Its layers, for example, write the age-long record of the seasons. There are thick layers of growth for good years and thin ones when there was drought or a cool season. By counting back from the outside, it is possible to figure out the date of each year so recorded.

An ancient tree on a hillside has gone through many dangers. The outstanding difference between animal and vegetable life is the fact that most animals can move and most plants cannot. The tree is firmly fastened to one spot. No matter what happens, it cannot run away. It must stay right there and see all emergencies through. Maybe, when this monarch was one hundred fifty years old, there was a forest fire that severely seared one side of it. The burn would leave a scar which would be covered up by the putting on of later cloaks of growth. Digging into the log would show the record of this burn, and counting the rings would reveal its date.

The flint heads of arrows might be found embedded deep in the body of such a tree. They might mean that a battle of the tribes was fought here and the date of the fight could be set down. It might have taken place before Columbus came and would show the sort of weapons then in use. Or a spot might be found far in the tree where a blaze had been slashed down its side. Back of this blaze might be found half a dozen leaden bullets. This might mean that a white man had passed this way and done some practice shooting with the blaze as the target. So might a record of the coming of the white man be written, with the date. A great storm might have blown in 1532, tearing big branches from this tree. It would heal over the wounds that were made, but would leave the mark and date. A plague of boring insects would leave their record. They might be wiped out by the coming of hordes of woodpeckers and these in turn would write their story in the body of the tree. Thus it comes about, strangely, that historical facts reaching through centuries may set themselves down deep in the bodies of trees where they can be dug out by men who patiently delve as do those who attempt to read the hieroglyphics of ancient Egypt.

The oldest individuals and the tallest of all plants in the world belong to the pine family. The Big Trees of California, whose proper name is *sequoia* and whose blood sisters are the redwoods, are cousins to the spruce, the fir, and the cedar, and are cone bearers. All the members of this family are of an old order of plants, but the Big Trees are its most striking survival. They typify the world as it existed before the glaciers came down from the north and changed the vegetation of the earth —the age when vegetation grew rank, and plants and animals were of giant size. In all the world these preglacial trees have survived only in California. There they stand, monsters whose trunks are thirty feet across, whose crests reach to a height of 350 feet. They dwarf the forest trees about them as an elephant, which is an animal survival of an old order, dwarfs cows, horses, and sheep of the barnyard. Individual trees have stood still for four or five thousand years and have seen generations of other forest neighbors come and go. These specimens of the vegetation of an earlier age, surviving only in small numbers on the Pacific slope, have been taken all around the world, and specimens of this rarest and most spectacular of plants may now be found growing on the shores of Lake Geneva, in Switzerland, or at the foot of the Italian Alps, or in many other places where rare trees are cultivated.

The bald cypress, a tree related to the true cypress, is

A DOUGLAS FIR TREE GROWN OVER 250 FEET TALL

the member of the pine family that can stand with its feet in water and still get along quite well, an ability possessed by few trees. There are bald cypress swamps from Delaware to Texas. The water seems to have a strange effect on the bases of these trees, causing them to flare out near its surface. The roots, too, act queerly. They buckle up and form "knees" that look for all the world like those which a man makes when he sits on the ground and pulls his feet up under him. No one knows why these roots, growing unnaturally in the water, act so strangely, but the theory is that they are trying to get above the water for breathing purposes. Another peculiarity of the bald cypress is the fact that, despite its evergreen relationships, it sheds its leaves in winter.

The red cedar is a pine cousin that, with its western cousins, is to be found in every state in the Union. Growing in soils good or bad, it furnishes a bushy, rugged evergreen mop that decorates almost any scene upon which American eyes are likely to look, provides winter quarters for the hardy birds that refuse to be driven south by the snows, furnishes the wood from which lead pencils are made, the material for pleasantly scented cedar chests, and fence posts for the farmer that long defy decay.

Loved by man as are few trees, planted by him as an ornament to his driveways and as a silent watcher over the graves of his ancestors, the red cedar none the less finds itself mixed up in a situation that spells tragedy similar to that which has befallen the white pine, and turns the hand of its benefactor against it and in places leads to its sure destruction. It harbors the apple rust, another mushroom outlaw. It must often be destroyed that the apple crop may be saved.

Finally, there is the Douglas fir, massed on the mountain slopes that border the Pacific in Washington and

Oregon. It stands in dense woods, trees three feet, six feet, sometimes ten feet in diameter, with trunks like the spars of ships, straight and tall, the finest forests of the best structural timber in all the world. Often the forests of Douglas fir are pure with no other timber intermixed. Sometimes Sitka spruce is present, another splendid tree of the pine family. It is taller than the Douglas fir and its wood is light and strong and therefore especially fitted for use in airplane building.

The nobility of the trees of this family as specimens of the handiwork of Nature is unsurpassed. In their usefulness to man in his need of timber with which to build his many structures, they are without a rival. They are a strong, splendid tribe, coming down through the ages, sometimes set down as the first family of the vegetable world.

CHAPTER XXII

STRONG MAN OAK

THE OAK is the strong man of the tree brotherhood. It has often been called the king of the forest, just as the maple, symbol of grace and beauty, is styled its queen. It has a rugged and sturdy trunk, harsh and crooked limbs, a stocky base, and a tap root that is giant strong below ground. It grips the earth and challenges the fiercest of storms to shake it loose. So sturdy is it that it may live on a hillside 1,000 years, even 2,000 years.

The oak stands like a rugged wrestler with knotted muscles challenging all comers. Whoever saw an uprooted oak or one with its trunk snapped off in the wind! The heart of the oak is a symbol of strength. Whenever man wants timber that is hard and enduring, he cuts it from the oak tree. There are cathedrals in Europe that were built a thousand years ago in which the oak timbers are as strong today as when first put in. Ax handles, wagon wheels, the ribs of lifeboats, are made of oak.

Oak trees, wherever found in all the world, carry their trade-mark with them. That trade-mark is the acorn. Every oak everywhere comes from and produces this acorn sitting tightly in its cup until it is ripe. No tree on earth that is not an oak bears acorns. Acorns and oaks are never separated. If you are wondering whether a tree in the forest is an oak, look for acorns on it or beneath it, or for acorn cups clinging to its branches after the fruit has fallen out of them. Some trees bear fruit, some berries, some beans, but the oak is known by its acorns. These acorns are oak seed from which new generations of trees will grow and are therefore of greater use than a mere trade-mark.

Oak leaves are usually quite different from those of other trees because they are marked by deep scallops, by notches and bays as if a child of the age that likes to cut out with scissors had been at work on them. The general shape of the oak leaf is oval, but different species have different patterns cut into their sides. But while most leaves have these deep bays in them, sometimes cutting them almost in two, all oak leaves are not irregular. In Southern forests, for instance, there is a smooth green tree with a leafy top and regular oblong leaves that is likely to puzzle the tree lover. The leaves are for all the world like those of a willow tree, but none of its habits are those of the willow. And there upon its branches are growing some of the finest specimens of acorns that one would care to see. They prove, of course, that it is an oak tree. Because of the shape of its leaves, it is called the willow oak. It is just now becoming popular for park and street planting. The shingle oak, a wide-spread tree, has a leaf much like that

EVERY TREE ON WHICH AN ACORN GROWS IS AN OAK

of the peach tree. Live oaks which in the South and the West attempt to be evergreens, also have smooth-edged leaves. All these leaves, to be sure, are stiff and glossy, with leather-like faces and of an oak type. The tree, however, cannot be identified easily by the shape of its leaves as they are commonly known. The acorn provides the test.

The oaks are not a plant family in themselves. There are two other cup-bearing cousins that must be put in with them. One of these is the beech and the other is the chestnut. The family takes its name from the beeches, which, to be sure, are of much less importance than the oaks. The three make up the beech family in the botanist's division of the plant world. The three cousins taken together are the mast-bearing trees—"mast" being the nuts and acorns that they produce. This mast is often valuable to man. In many parts of the country hogs are fattened on mast in the autumn, and this food is thought to give their meat a flavor that is better than any other.

There is only one kind of beech tree native to the United States, where there are fifty kinds of oaks. It is a beautiful, straight-limbed, smooth, well-groomed tree that always gathers many youngsters of its kind about it. These come from the beechnuts that the squirrels and blue jays scatter about for it. The chestnut tree is a great, spreading fellow, producing its prickly burs. It has long, tapering leaves and an elegant bearing. These most refined cupbearers are probably ashamed of their rough oak cousin, but he, none the less, is much more important than are they.

THE OAK TREE IS KNOWN BY ITS LEAVES AND ACORNS

Of the fifty different kinds of native oaks in the United States, about half live on one side of the Rocky Mountains and half on the other. The mountains set up a barrier that these trees could not cross, and so there are certain differences between Eastern and Western oaks. But whether in the East or in the West, there are two plain divisions among the oak. This difference lies in whether they ripen their acorns in one year or in two. The white oaks bloom in the spring, set their acorns and ripen them in time for the squirrel harvest that very autumn. Their limbs are bare of acorns through the winter. The other breed, the black oak, starts out in the same way in the spring, but the acorns are only half-grown when autumn arrives. They stick on their trees through the winter and the following summer. They are not fully developed as squirrel food until the second autumn arrives.

There are certain other plain differences between these two groups. The white oaks have light-colored bark and the black oaks are dark. The lobes of the leaves of white oaks have round corners. They never tend to prick as do holly leaves. The leaves of black oaks, that take two years to develop their acorns, have sharp corners. There are spiny points on them that tend to be prickly. The acorns of white oaks are sweet, while those of black oaks are bitter. This latter point makes it more likely that man or beast would eat white oak acorns than black oak acorns. It may be because of this that there are ten times as many black oaks as white oaks.

The greatest of all oaks is a member of this first group and itself known individually as the white oak. There

TREE CLAIMED TO BE THE OLDEST LIVE OAK

is a handsome specimen of it on each side of the Rockies. It is a splendid, upstanding tree, sometimes one hundred fifty feet tall and eight feet through the trunk. Its heavy, tough wood has proved so popular that the lumberman has come near destroying the good specimens of it. Like most of the oaks, it grows tall in the forest, where it must go up for light, and spreads wide when it lives in the open. Its rugged arms are crooked and strong. They trace many fancy patterns against the wintry skyline when they are bare. Their summer leaves are slim, with deep notches in them. They let the sunlight past until it reaches far in toward the heart of the tree. This makes it possible for other leaves to grow deep in the tree.

The post oak is a familiar member of the white oak group which ripens its acorns the first year. It is a sprawling, sturdy fellow, all angles and elbows, fifty or sixty feet high and broad at the top. Its leaf is thick and leathery, with three or five square lobes. Seen from a distance, the post oak tree in summer looks almost black. Its leaves, seared by the frosts of winter, do not fall off as soon as other leaves, but remain as a drab screen to its knotty limbs. Most winter American landscapes are likely to present brown splotches that are made by some oak tree that clings to its leaves after they are dead.

This post oak tree offers itself in a stern usefulness to man. It furnishes the best of railroad ties which when exposed to earth and moisture, are slow to decay. It supplies sturdy barrel staves that inclose much of the sugar of the world.

The bur oak has a rough cup that covers the greater part of its acorn. This is one of the big oaks of the East, sometimes one hundred seventy feet tall and with wide-flung branches. It is indeed a sturdy giant. Its leaves are often a foot long. They make a dense shade in contrast with the more open effect produced by the leaves of many oaks. The bur oak breaks the prairies of the West, shelters the barnyards of Pennsylvania, and glories in the rigorous winters of Maine.

The chestnut oak with a leaf like the chestnut tree, but with annual acorns that prove its breed, thrives around New York City. It follows the Alleghenies to the South and finds its greatest glory in Tennessee. There is a chestnut oak still standing at Fishkill-on-the-Hudson under which General Washington regularly mounted his horse when encamped there during the Revolutionary War. It was an old tree then, but is still hale and hearty.

There would seem to be a bit of confusion in naming the members of the black oak group that takes two years to ripen its acorns. One of these black oaks, for example, is called the red oak. It comes near matching the white oak for size. It is round-topped, heavy-leafed, and handsome for planting in parks. It is a strictly American oak, but the English early began to take it overseas for planting. Many specimens of it are now to be seen in European parks. There it flames out in brilliant autumn colors, a trick which native European trees do not seem to know. The red oak lends itself readily to being transplanted from the forest to the city street and so is crowding in on the skyscraper.

The scarlet oak is another member of the black oak group. It is the tallest, slenderest, most graceful of the oaks. Of them all, it lights the most brilliant torch when trees are blazing forth at the touch of frost. Its leaves are paper thin and the bays in them are bigger than the lobes. Thus are they quite fairylike when compared with the heavy, foot-long leaves of the bur oak. The scarlet oak is growing always more popular for city planting.

Hardiest of a hardy race is the mountain live oak of

the Pacific coast, which furnishes tough timber for making wagons and farm implements in that part of the world. It is a creature of the wilds which clings to canyon sides and sinks its roots into deep crevasses in the rocks. It would scorn being crowded by other trees in a forest. It must stand alone, that its branches may spread wide. A mountain live oak may be fifty feet high and one hundred feet wide. It refuses to come lower down the mountains than 2,000 feet above the sea level. From there it scrambles always upward. As conditions grow severer at the higher altitudes, it decreases in size. At 9,000 feet above the sea it is found as a tiny oak tree, still carrying the acorn trade-mark, that reaches but a foot in height. Half-grown acorns, clinging to its branches amidst the snows of winter, show that it is of the black oak group.

The pin oak is among the most popular of forest trees for transplanting to city streets. Its slender beauty and its shadowy leaves are much like those of the scarlet oak, but it has plain markings of its own. It is easy to recognize along the city streets of the nation, where it is becoming so plentiful. The pin oak has a form that makes it easy to tell it from other trees. Its trunk, wide at the base, is likely to rise straight as a pillar for fifteen or twenty feet without a branch. It tapers gracefully, as perfect as a ship's spar. Few trees have a more beautiful base than the pin oak. The limbs that are lowest down are longer than those higher up. The length of the branches decreases gradually as one goes higher up the trunk. Thus the tree becomes an inverted cone, coming to a point at the top as do many of the members

CLOSE-UP OF THE STURDY OAK TRUNK

of the pine family. The pin oak is the only oak built to this pattern. There are few trees of this shape in the woods or along the roadsides. The cone form is a fairly safe indication that a shade tree which is not of the pine group is a pin oak.

When the branches of this tree are bare in the winter, the small twigs that bear leaves for a while and then die may be seen. Crisscrossed throughout the tree they look like so many pins and give the tree its name. One objection to the pin oak is the fact that, as it grows older, there is likely to be a good deal of deadwood inside its outer rim of green leaves.

City life is very hard on the children of the forest, and few of them live long as part of it. Accident is likely to wound the city tree and weaken its trunk or roots. When storms howl among city buildings, their currents are given directions and twists that are much more likely to break trees down than if they were standing in the open or among their fellows in the woods. Soft-wood trees, quick to grow, such as the silver maple, often find their trunks weakened by the wounds that come from city life. As a result they are strewn across city streets after every storm.

The lusty oak, be it red oak or pin oak, deep-rooted, strong-trunked, defies the rough usage which city trees receive. The attacks of insects injure it little. It does not require much pruning. Treacherous city winds are seldom strong enough to break its sturdy stalk. It thrives in its little squares of earth surrounded by city pavements. An automobile may smash itself against an oak tree, and the wounds it makes will heal without weakening its trunk. The oak survives in city streets where other trees die. So it is coming to pass that those in charge of tree planting, who act wisely, set out many oaks. And the favorites among these are red oaks and pin oaks. In the city of Washington in late years, for example, nearly all the planting has been of these two varieties. They stand like endless lines of solemn sentinels along the handsome street vistas of the nation's capital.

THE SALTY WATER FROM ICE CREAM FREEZERS KILLS THE TREES IN FRONT OF DRUG STORES

Other problems faced by those responsible for trees along city or village streets arise as incidents to business. Who has not passed along streets and seen sturdy trees that showed no injury on the surface gradually sicken and die? It is a strange thing that these trees are usually in front of drug stores. It is hard for a tree standing in front of a drug store to keep alive. This is because drug stores serve ice cream. It is not the ice cream, however, that kills the trees, but the salt that is packed about it in the freezer.

Druggists do not seem to know that salt kills trees. Possibly most of the blame should be charged up to the ice-cream makers. Their wagons stop in front of drug stores and other establishments that serve ice cream. They leave and take away freezers. They repack ice cream. They spill salt in doing so. The druggist's boy often rolls a freezer from which the ice cream has been used out to the curb and empties the salty water from it at the base of a tree. This need not be done many times before the tree is as effectually killed as though it had been chopped down. Yet few druggists or other people seem to know why these trees die.

It has often been remarked that "great oaks from little acorns grow." Strange to say, one rarely hears anything about the growth of the acorn and how it comes to pass. Knowing the way of plants, he is likely to surmise that the development of this smooth and graceful tree seed had its start with a flower. This is true, but there are unusual points about the flowers of oak trees that call for explaining.

Many trees make a great show by putting out their blossoms in early spring before their leaves appear. The magnolia tree with its huge blooms makes an early display. The locust tree quite covers itself with clusters of flowers which remind even those who cannot see, of their presence by sending out a sweet and cloying odor. But the mighty oak is modest in its blooming. It waits until its leaves are coming out and these go far toward hiding the flowers. Those who have watched oak trees in the spring know that they hang out clusters of catkins, like so many tassels, along their smaller twigs. Not many learn, however, that these are not the real flowers of the oaks. The catkins grow no acorns. These come from tiny and rarely noticed blooms hidden in among the leaves.

We have seen that there are male and female date and other trees. The two different flowers needed to produce dates as seeds for new plants grow on different trees. In the case of the oak and many others, both kinds of flowers grow on the same tree. But to make seed, the pollen of the one must get into the other to fertilize it. On the oak the catkins furnish the pollen. It gets into the air and the wind drifts it into the little acorn flowers not far away at the bases of the leaves. There it plants its spark of life, and little acorns grow from which great oaks may in the end develop.

But there is another chapter in the life story of the oak that is worth sketching in. The acorn must, of course, get itself planted or it cannot produce a tree. We have seen the many devices to which plants resort to get their seeds scattered about. An acorn dropped here and there gets its feet into the soil and grows of itself. A very small percentage of oak trees, however, are started in this accidental manner. Most of them come from acorns for which holes have been very carefully dug and into which the earth has been tamped on top of them. These acorns have been as carefully smoothed over as the hyacinth bulb that is tucked away in the city back yard.

This precise task has been performed by none other than the squirrel of the woods, without the help of which oak trees and nut trees would cease to exist in the forests. Walnuts, hickories, pecans, and other nut trees are not in the immediate family of the acorn producers. They are not so distantly related, however, and they join with the acorn trees in their dependence upon the squirrel in getting planted.

It is the gray squirrel that does most of the planting.

The red squirrel is more likely to hide its nuts away in a hollow log or under the barn, where they have little chance of growing into trees. But the gray squirrel has a different way of laying in his winter supply of food.

In the autumn when the nuts and acorns are falling, the gray squirrel works early and late. He selects his acorns with great care, testing each to make sure that it is sound and without worms. He picks out good places on the floor of the forest, digs holes four inches deep, plants his acorns and covers them up. For weeks he is busy with this work. He plants hundreds of acorns. Then he goes back to his nest in an old woodpecker hole in the trunk of a great tree and goes to sleep. He lives rather quietly through the winter, but is not one of those animals whose sleep is unbroken through the months. He comes out now and again for an airing and for food. He digs up one by one the acorns he has buried and devours them.

SQUIRRELS PLANT THE ACORNS FROM WHICH OAK TREE FORESTS GROW

The marvel of it is that he can find them. With the appearance of the floor of the forest entirely changed, with a foot of snow on the ground, the gray squirrel is still able to locate the spot where he buried every acorn. He can be seen to go from place to place, to dig through the snow, into the ground, and come up with an acorn in his mouth.

But he does not get them all. Perhaps he has planted more than he needs. Perhaps he fails to find one here and there. Thus it comes about that certain acorns and nuts find themselves nicely planted when the spring showers and warm days come. They sprout, and it is thus that "great oaks from little acorns grow." But not enough of them would ever start on their way to keep their kind alive in the forests if it were not for the help of the squirrels.

So the nut-bearing trees and the squirrels have established a sort of partnership that helps them both. As a matter of fact, the very life of both depend upon it. If the squirrels did not get nuts, they would starve. If they should disappear, they would be much missed by members of the man tribe. Squirrels get along better with man than almost any other wild animal. They are able to live near him even in the great cities. They are the closest tie between city dwellers and wild animal life. On the other hand if the squirrel did not pay the nut trees for its food by planting new crops of them, they would lose out in the fight they carry on with other plants for a place on the hillside. And man would be deprived of the nuts of the forest that come to his table.

Chapter XXIII

THE STATELY ELM

ONE COULD hardly write of shade trees and fail to give space to the stately American elm. As the oak is today proving its mastery in the crowded city, the elm long ago established itself as the monarch that should span the village street and best display its grandeur as a solitary figure beside the country road.

Seen at its best, standing alone on a hillside in New England or Pennsylvania or Michigan, it is likely to cause the observer to pause and ask himself if this is not the handsomest tree that grows anywhere beneath the sun. In its proper sphere, there is no doubt but that it is the greatest of all shade trees.

If the season is summer, what is seen at a distance in looking at an elm is a colossal trunk that might be a column which supports a fountain of the giants that bubbles and spills over in graceful sprays of living green. The whole presents a living globe a hundred feet high and as far across, with swinging branches at the outer edges that suggest sprays of falling water. The sphere sways and dimples with the breeze. Every oblong, straight-ribbed leaf, hung on its slender stem, stirs in the wind and lends life to the picture.

If the season is winter, the tree has lost none of its

beauty. The tracings of the bare limbs of it are such as to suggest the lines of a Gothic cathedral. The column of its trunk rises sturdily for a dozen feet, then it divides into five or six parts, and these climb upward, spreading but slowly outward. They in turn branch, and the larger group reaches up and up, tending outward. Toward the end of their spans they throw out sprays that bend outward and droop slowly toward the ground. The effect is that of a huge vase that spills its garlands in an orderly manner on all sides. Fringelike they hang, swaying in the wind, as graceful as the lace on a young girl's parasol. They invite the Baltimore oriole, brilliant in yellow and black, to bind their flowing twigs together, as is the way of the hangbird, and weave its nest among them. There it may swing through summer days, suspended so far out that not even the robber squirrel can climb to it for a taste of eggs for breakfast.

There could be no greater contrast than that between the slim, graceful, sweeping, orderly behavior of the branches of an elm tree and the harsh, knotty, angular, bendings and twistings of the limbs of a gnarled oak.

The oak and the elm, it may as well be said, are open rivals for the admiration of tree lovers in the north temperate zone all around the world. The one is a symbol of rugged strength. The method of the other is that of sweeping grace. Each is a masterpiece in the realm of trees at the feet of which puny man may lay tributes in accordance with his tastes.

There were both oaks and elms in the Old World where the ancestors of Americans dwelt and developed. Ancient druids are said to have favored groves of oak trees as furnishing a canopy beneath which they might worship. The Norseman, however, was before them in assigning a nobler rôle to the elm. Odin, the God of Heaven, according to Norse mythology, selected the branch of an elm from which to fashion the first woman.

THE LEAFY ELM IN SUMMER IS THE GREATEST OF SHADE TREES

There were elm trees in Europe, and early settlers in America knew them well and prized them as shade trees about their homes. It was because of this that they planted elms up and down the early New England streets. But this American elm was of a different breed than those across the sea. The grace and sweep of branches, the creation of the fountain of green, was beyond that of any of its kin. The European elms are stiffer and more oak-like. So are many of the thirteen varieties of America. But that tree which is known as the American elm is so much greater than all the rest that it is the tree that is usually meant when people speak of elms.

This was the tree that was planted along the village streets of New England. Time has developed these plantings into aged trees that have come to their handsomest maturity. Although the streets they border are sixty to eighty feet wide, the sweeping elm branches from either side have met over them, and those who travel them today pass beneath an unbroken canopy of green. Some of these villages have developed into cities and are still dominated by the elm. New Haven is known as the "city of elms." Concord, Andover, and Salem pass the generations beneath their branches. At Cambridge, Massachusetts, the old elm still stands under which Washington took command of the American army. The day Burgoyne was brought in a prisoner during the Revolutionary War, an elm was planted in Albany, New York, and it stands today, marking an event in history. Two splendid elms, named Paul and Virginia, stand on the bank of the Susquehanna River at Wilkes-Barre, Pennsylvania, and are widely prized. In Georgia, not long ago, a spreading elm was deeded the plot of land on which it stood, that no man would have the right to disturb it. In front of the White House in Washington a number of splendid elms "lift their leafy arms to pray."

In New England the American elm is more highly prized than elsewhere. New England claims the elm as her own, although it may be found all the way to the Rockies, and the specimens are equally good in many other states. But the elm early found its place in the

New England landscape and has come to be associated with it.

As a shade tree, the elm fits ideally into certain situations and not so well into others. So large is it, so great is the spread of its branches, that it must have room. In the row these trees should be planted sixty to eighty feet apart. Planted at the curb in a city street with tall buildings near by, they could not grow naturally without poking their branches into office windows. As a matter of fact, they would lean out toward the street, seeking sunlight, and become crooked and lopsided structures. In smoky cities, even when planted in parks, they do not flourish, because their leaves are rough and the soot sticks to them. Thus are they smothered where the glossy leaf of the oak is little affected.

LEAVES OF THE AMERICAN ELM

The elm must have a chance to fling its limbs. In the village streets, planted not too closely together, with the houses sitting back from the curb, it grows into its splendid, leafy corridors. Standing by itself at the end of a park vista, beside a lonely country road, or clustered about farm buildings, it is a patriarch without a peer, undisputed master among trees whose purpose is to furnish shade.

Although the elm is a tree beneath which many people walk during all the years of their lives, not many of them know about the manner of its flowering. Its vast array of blooms open with no great blaze of color high over the heads of passers-by and are little noticed. This flowering comes about in the early spring before the leaves begin to appear. The oak blooms follow the leaves, but those of the elm go ahead of them. Even during the winter the elm shows its buds of two classes. There are round, fat buds which are for the flowers, and slim, pointed buds which are for leaves. Early in the spring those people who walk along streets that are bordered by elms find them sprinkled with paper-like scales which, although they may not understand it, have been dropped by the elm flowers far above. The appearance of these scales on the ground might be taken as a summons to the passer-by to look for the great flowering that is going on overhead. A look upward will reveal a wine-colored tint throughout the tree. An examination of an overhanging branch will show the abundant clusters of purplish, brownish, reddish, flowers. It is a surprise to learn that the elm produces such an array of flowers. They are converting the spraying branches of the tree into a huge, but mild-tinted, bouquet. The tree that is built like a vase has come into its own.

Six weeks later those who stroll beneath the elms are given another reminder of transformations that are going on overhead. The pavement is again sprinkled with a product of the branches above. This time the offering takes the form of a roundish disk, half an inch across, thin at the edges but with an object at the center that may be of importance. It is of importance to the elm, for it is the seed, carrying the germ of life from which other elms may spring. This roundish disk with the thin edges is the device which the elm uses to get its seeds scattered. It forms a light, airy particle that is likely to flutter much and carry far in the wind.

The elm asks the wind to do for it what the squirrel does for the oak. It would seem an easier way to get its seed planted.

IN THE EARLY SPRING THE ELM TREE BECOMES A HUGE BOUQUET WITH THESE PURPLISH FLOWERS ON EVERY TWIG

Yet an elm tree may make a million seeds a year for a century and release them on the wind and still do only the work that is necessary to hold the balance in the woods. If ten per cent of the elm seeds grew, this tree would overrun the world in a generation. The tree makes this vast number of seeds because the chances are so slim that any one of them will ever grow into a tree. Among birds, the swift-winged doves need lay only two eggs at nesting time to keep their race alive. The partridge, living on the ground and poor at flight, must lay sixteen. The number of eggs a bird lays is the measure of the chance its young one has of living to be grown. So it is with the trees. So slight are the chances of individual seeds ever to grow to be trees that millions must be released by single specimens or the race will die out. So it is with the elm.

Trees are not likely to be given much attention in the wintertime. They stand bare and still, giving no evidence of life. It is life and action that is interesting, and

THE ELM IN WINTER SHOWS ITS VASELIKE FORM

so the winter trees are not noticed. But there is beauty in them if one stops for a look. There is a plan of architecture in every tree just as there is in every building along a city street. Often the bare outlines of branches are designs of great beauty. This is particularly true of the mighty elm. Its formation of a huge vase out of which sweeps the slim lines of its arching limbs is most pleasing to the artist.

The bare tree, standing there in the winter snow, is a live and vital thing, awaiting the first gun of spring to start its outpouring of flower and leaf. How different from the dead tree, its bark sagging, its branches out of order, does it look! It is still wrapped in its blanket of cambium, or inner bark, through which the sap circulates and feeds every twig. It is through this inner bark, and other layers of wood just beneath it, that the sap will begin to surge when springtime comes.

But the moisture in this cambium freezes solid when the thermometer goes low. Take a living bud, already formed on the tree, and cut it open out of doors when the thermometer is ten degrees above zero. Look at it under a microscope. The ice crystals can be plainly seen. Yet this tender bud, at this stage of its development, is not injured by freezing. But let warm days come late in the winter and cause the sap to flow out into the buds. Let spring growth get under way. Then let it turn cold again. Such tender blossoms as those of the peach tree are likely to be killed and the fruit crop damaged.

Most people suppose that buds are grown in the spring just before they appear as leaves or flowers. As a matter of fact, they are then a year old. They have been forming under the skin of the tree through all the season that has gone before. Whenever a leaf grows on a twig, it starts at its base a bud that is to take its place when it is gone. This bud develops through the summer while the leaf is in its glory. When the leaf is ready to fall, the twig draws from it whatever it has that may furnish food for the bud it leaves behind. After the leaf falls, the buds take form, and store up that food against the coming of spring. All winter they sleep and wait. When the spring comes, they slowly awake to the warmth of it and begin to bestir themselves for their busy season. The sap which carries the building materials up to the buds begins to flow. The tree, through the winter, has manufactured none of this. It is made by the leaves after they become green and turn themselves to the sun. It is then that they manufacture the starch and sugar that feeds the tree. The growth of the early spring must be drawn from the reserves stored up from the year before. All that early glory of flower, bud and leaf, is built from this reserve, carried up and out through the sap elevators. Finally, when the cloth of green is fully spread, the sugar factories in the leaves running full blast, growth is at its height, and the tree is most alive.

CHAPTER XXIV

THE MAPLE TREE

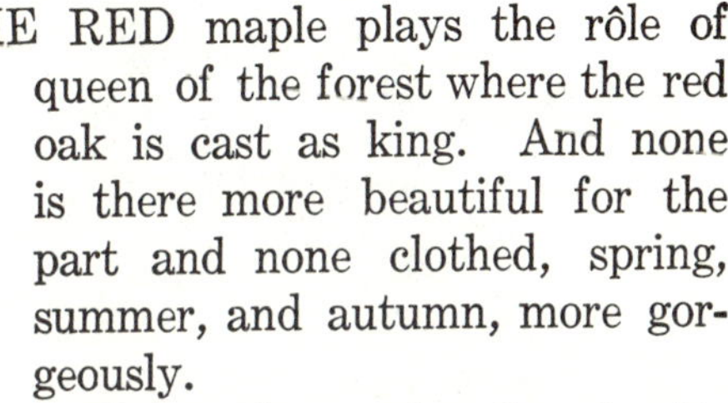

THE RED maple plays the rôle of queen of the forest where the red oak is cast as king. And none is there more beautiful for the part and none clothed, spring, summer, and autumn, more gorgeously.

The red maple flaunts its colors even in the early spring when it has merely bare branches and twigs to show. Its tiny twigs are even then a bright red, brighter than they will be later on. The buds of promise that stud them are as red as rubies. It is one of the earliest trees to flower in the spring and when its blooms come they, too, are red. They lend a ruddy glow to the entire tree top. They cluster about the bare twigs before the leaves begin to appear in the early spring. The leaves themselves are red in their youth. A few weeks later the "keys" that dangle from their branches and hold the maple seed are red. Then in the autumn, when the leaves approach the time when they will wave their final good-bys to the summer scenes which they have gladdened, they change again to scarlet in honor of their queen.

There are many who argue that the maple is the handsomest of trees. Certainly there is no other that lends the richness of coloring of its autumn leaves. And of all

THE POPULAR BUT NONE TOO STABLE SILVER MAPLE

the maples, that which earns the name of "red," sometimes also called the swamp maple because of its love of the lowlands, is the handsomest. And a sturdy hardwood tree it is withal.

The silver maple is more widely known in America than any other. It borders river banks throughout most of North America. When its seeds are dropped in May, they immediately spring up, and by September many sturdy little trees are started on their way. Plant them anywhere, and they proceed promptly and with little care to develop into trees. The silver maple is a quick grower and a soft-wood tree. It is also a tree of short life. It may grow to be 120 feet high. Its branches are long and spreading. Its leaf is the most beautiful of them all, cut with its deep indentations and lined with the light tints of its silver.

But the silver maple does not possess the sturdy traits of most of the members of its family. Its quick growth and soft wood are responsible for its weakness of character. It is like the North Carolina poplar or the cottonwood of the West. It grows quickly but does not endure. It will not stand up under the pressure of city life. They are the silver maples that lie across city streets after every storm.

Despite its weaknesses, this tree has been planted in greater numbers on city streets than almost any other. This is because it is so attractive in appearance, because it is so easily grown, because it produces shade so quickly. Offering these inducements, it has appealed to people who have not known the life cycles of trees, and few people did so in the days of our fathers.

Nowadays those who wisely plant trees in cities and towns think many decades ahead. They have gathered information about the lives of trees and their deportment as they grow older. They have learned that soft woods and soft-wooded varieties are not safe for planting. They know that it takes many times the care to grow a red

DEVELOPING LEAVES AND KEYS OF THE RED MAPLE

maple than it does a silver maple, but that the tree that results is worth the extra trouble.

The leaf of the maple is of course, its trade-mark. There are few leaves that are more familiar. The botanist will tell you that this leaf is "palmately veined and lobed." This means that it is built on the plan of the palm of the hand. It branches out into three or five lobes that might be compared to the fingers. In the red-maple leaf there are three lobes and the leaf is roundish. In the silver maple the leaves are slimmer with their five lobes more distinct. In the sugar maple the fingers are farther apart, and the leaf is more solid in appearance.

All maples have the keys as an additional trade-mark. The wings of the keys may be of different lengths and tints in different maples, but there is never any question about the family of the trees from which they come.

The most famous of all the maples, doubtless, is the sugar maple, also called the rock maple. It has the distinction of being one of the handsomest trees in all the world. It grows large, strong, shapely, verdant, glorious in its autumn coloring. Its trunk is of hard wood and sturdy. It will live through the generations. It yields maple sugar and maple sirup to tickle the palates of a nation. It is a handsome shade tree for transplanting to parks and city streets.

The sugar maple is not often thought of as a shade tree of surpassing beauty. Because it is a worker that yields a product that has value in dollars and cents, it is always considered from the standpoint of the cakes of maple sugar it delivers year after year. But if it were not a producer of sugar it would be rated on the basis of its beauty as a tree for forest and park, and would take high rank.

Often in the late summer the sugar maple flings out a single branch like a scarlet flag among the green. Sometimes half the branches of the tree will turn red. Those who do not know the sugar maple may come to the conclusion that something is wrong, that this is a dying tree. Such, however, is not the fact. The sugar maple is merely getting ahead of its fellows with the paint brush.

A peculiar thing about the brilliant colors which the American woods present in the autumn is the fact that woods elsewhere fail to produce effects that begin to compare with them. When Europeans come to America and see these autumn colors, they are greatly impressed by them. They furnish an element of beauty which does not exist on the other side of the ocean.

THE LEAF AND SEED OF THE SUGAR MAPLE

The business of getting sugar from the maple trees was inherited from the Indians. When white men came to America they found that the Iroquois Indians in particular made a great deal of the sugar they had learned to get from the sap of these beautiful trees. In the springtime when the sap was beginning to run, they always held a great festival. When the crows began to appear, they started getting ready. They moved bag and baggage to the maple groves, carrying their utensils with them. They built temporary wigwams, brought their medicine men along for the incantations. A great dance was given and many charms were brought into play to induce the Holy Spirit to bring the warm weather that would start the sap to running.

The white man borrowed all that he could from the red man. For a long time the trees were tapped almost as crudely as had been done by the Indians. Only a generation ago the sap was boiled in an old-fashioned pot over an open fire in the woods. Nowadays a bricked-in oven and a patented evaporator are generally present.

Before the snow is entirely gone from the ground, the maple-sugar farmer begins to tap his trees. He bores holes in them with a three-quarter-inch auger and hangs buckets in such a way that they will catch the sap as it trickles out of a spigot driven into the hole. As the spring sunshine begins to warm the tree, the sap begins to flow. To be sure, the flow is very slow. In the middle of the day when it is at its best, it gets as high as seventy drops a minute. The drops keep coming for three weeks and in that time a good maple-sugar tree is likely to yield as much as twenty-five gallons of sap. This, when boiled down into sugar, is likely to amount to about five pounds. There are many maple-sugar farms in Vermont and New Hampshire that produce 1,000 pounds of maple sugar each season. There is one near Sanford, New York, that yields around 5,000 pounds of maple sugar each year.

Of the maples that have come to be favorites for street planting, however, the honor goes to a foreigner. The Norway maple is an immigrant. It is a hard wood which nevertheless grows quite rapidly. It is a graceful, round-headed tree with dense foliage. It turns yellow in the

THE RED MAPLE BEFORE APPEARANCE OF FOLIAGE

autumn, but misses the brilliance of the American varieties. Its flowers, which are yellow, do not open until the leaves are out, in which respect it is again different from American varieties. Break a growing twig or leaf stem of the Norway maple and a milky juice flows out. American maple twigs do not give out a milky juice. The foreigner can be identified by this juice.

These Norway maples are splendid trees to plant forty-five feet apart along city streets. They are being very widely planted by those agencies that have carefully studied the subject. There are many delicate problems, however, in this tree planting, that must be borne in mind. This Norway maple, for example, must have high ground on which to stand. If a row of them is to be planted along a street and it runs through a hollow where the ground is low and damp, they will die out at those places. The native red maple, however, likes low ground. The maple row may be patched by planting red maples on the low ground, and for most of the year the difference will scarcely be noticed. To be sure, the red maple flowers will glow forth in the spring ahead of those of the yellow Norways. To be sure, the red maple will blaze more brilliantly in the autumn. But one may be substituted quite successfully for the other.

There are peculiarities of growth that attach to the sugar maple also. It should be borne in mind that its other name is rock maple. It grows on high and rocky soils. In Washington, the nation's capital, where these matters have been carefully studied for half a century, one finds a row of sugar maples planted along a street that climbs a steep, rocky hill where they make one of the prize avenues of trees of the city. It has been learned also that these trees, when planted along a paved street where the sunlight and heat are reflected strongly upon them, do not flourish.

The mountain maple, a smallish tree, lends its yellow and red to many a hill and makes it shine out in the landscape. The striped maple is likewise a mountain variety and gets its name from the fact that the bark cracks open as the tree grows, exposing new skin the color of which is different from that of the old bark. Side by side, these skins of two ages produce the effect of stripes.

Box elder is a maple, though its leaf is shaped like that of the ash tree. It is often called the ash-leaved maple. It will grow almost anywhere, ranging from a river bottom to an elevation of 6,000 feet. Its hardihood led settlers moving into the treeless regions of the West to plant it. They knew that they could depend on it to grow quickly. So it was broadcast. People formed a liking for it and have kept on planting it, although it is not a sturdy or long-lived tree and should not be planted. It rates with the silver maple as a type to avoid.

Probably the strangest maple tree of all the tribe has ceased to be a tree and has become a vine. It is found in the forests of Oregon. This strange maple seems to have started out bravely enough to be a tree like the rest of them. But it lacked strength of character. It did not have enough backbone to stand erect. It toppled over on its face and lay there. But it kept on growing. It became a vine that sprawled all over the place. But its leaves and its keys are as distinctly those of the maple as are those of the red or sugar or any other of these cousins.

The sycamore, which the scientists call the *plane tree,* is close kin to the maple. The form of its leaf indicates the relationship. It is one of the largest of the shade trees. It grows well in parks and on city streets. It deserves a greater popularity than it enjoys. The virtues of two other handsome shade trees, not related to the maple, might be mentioned in passing. Linden trees, with dense masses of leaves in midsummer, are handsome specimens for city planting. The Japanese ginkgo, its great branches shooting out plumelike in all directions, is a thing of beauty and brings variety to an American landscape.

The blaze of color that comes in the woods in the autumn, in which the maples play a leading part, has a meaning that does not appear. It is a great occasion when the trees prepare to part with the leaves that they have worn so proudly through the summer. The vital thing about those leaves has been the green that was in them. The greener a leaf is, the better it is able to do its work. It is the green that breaks up the rays of the sun and puts the power in them at work taking the carbon dioxide out of the air and using it for tree-building material. Wood is largely carbon and all this is taken out of the air by green leaves.

As summer advances, the leaves become less green. They slow down in their work. By the end of the summer they have begun to prepare their stems in such a way that they will break off when the proper time comes. At their bases they build two layers of corklike cells. Leaves in the autumn may be broken easily at the point where these cells join and the plan of it may be seen. Let them alone and in the end they of themselves will break off.

Chapter XXV

THE RUBBER TREE

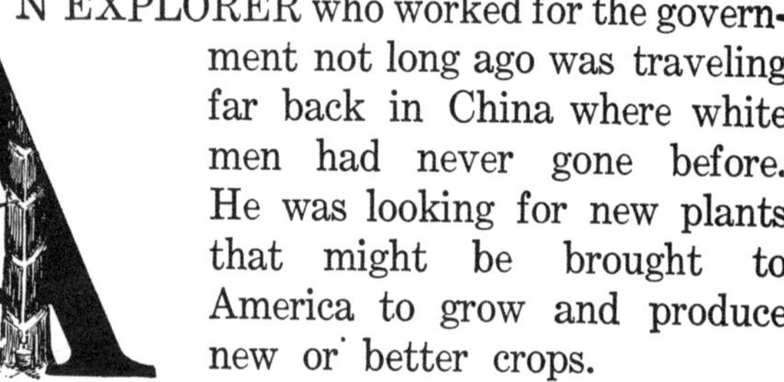

AN EXPLORER who worked for the government not long ago was traveling far back in China where white men had never gone before. He was looking for new plants that might be brought to America to grow and produce new or better crops.

One day he sat by the roadside with a group of natives about him. He took from his pocket a bundle of papers with a rubber band around it. He stretched this rubber band, let it slip off the papers, and draw itself up closely about his hand.

The natives stood in wonderment. They had never before seen anything that would stretch. They were frightened. Ignorant people are likely to think that there is witchcraft about whatever they cannot understand. They felt a great awe for this strange man with the band that was now long and now short.

Yet, strange to say, Julius Caesar never saw a rubber band. The knights of King Arthur's court probably would have been no less impressed than these Chinese had some visitor shown them one.

Much is made over the fact that potatoes, turkeys, tobacco, and many other products were not known in Europe before the discovery of America. Not much has been said about rubber in that connection. This may

RUBBER TREES IN A TROPICAL FOREST

be because rubber has not long been of any great importance.

It is true, nevertheless, that rubber is a gift of America to the world. Use was being made of it throughout the warm part of the western half of the world before the eastern half knew anything about it.

The Spaniards found, when they first came, that the natives of Mexico played a game with a ball which was made of a strange substance which caused it to bounce. This game was well worked out and well played. There were ball parks, even then, with seats for spectators. The newcomers found also that the natives of Mexico had a way of putting the material of which these balls were made on their coats and thus making them turn the rain. They also made bottles of it.

In South America this strange substance was much used. It was called *caoutchouc* (kōō'chŏŏk). This was a common name for it for a long time and it is still so called in a number of languages. It was 200 years later that an English chemist named Priestley, working in his laboratory, made an important discovery. He found that this caoutchouc would rub out marks made with a lead pencil. It soon came to be used for that purpose. It had already been used in making balls for children, but this was the first practical work that it had been set to do. Because it would erase lead-pencil marks, it came to be called *rubber*. Because it was from America, it was first styled Indian rubber and finally India rubber. It was called India rubber only a generation ago.

It was not until 1823 that another Briton, named MacIntosh, used rubber as the Mexicans had used it in making coats waterproof. Because of what he did, raincoats are still known all around the world as mackintoshes.

That rubber might be put on garments to make them turn the rain, it had to be changed into the form of a liquid. It took many years to find a liquid in which it might be dissolved. Finally, a hundred years ago, naphtha was developed and used. That was what MacIntosh employed. The garment was painted with naphtha with rubber in solution. The naphtha evaporated and the rubber stayed on.

But there was one bad thing about this rubber. It became soft and sticky when it was warm and hard when it was cold. It needed to be so improved that it would be the same all the time. There was need for hard rubber and for soft rubber. Some way should be found to make it hard or soft as needed.

It was an American named Goodyear who solved this problem in 1839. His has been an important name in the rubber industry ever since. Goodyear experimented with rubber mixed with sulphur. He could not get the results he wanted, however, until one day he accidentally spilled some of his mixture on a hot stove. It fused into a new material. A process of fusing rubber and sulphur called vulcanizing was developed. By varying this process many kinds of rubber could be produced. From these experiments, many objects have come to be made of rubber, such as rubber shoes, rubber gloves, hot-water bottles, mats, hose, tires, golf balls, brushes, stamps.

Natives of tropical America made rubber out of the juice of a tree. There were several trees that yielded this juice, but the greatest of them was the Hevea tree of Brazil. It grew and still grows, all through the rich lowlands of the Amazon Valley. The natives there, long before the white man came, knew quite well how to get the rubber from it. The rubber from the Amazon came to be known as Para rubber because Para was the port at the mouth of the river from which it was shipped. Para rubber from the Hevea tree ruled the rubber market. The Hevea is the tree of importance in the rubber world.

HOME OF THE RUBBER GATHERER IN BRAZIL

This Hevea tree belongs to a family that is not very well known in the North. It is called the *spurge family*. It registers its trade-mark in the way it puts up its seeds. There are three of these, each as big as the last joint of your thumb, bound closely together in a round pod. This seed pod has a trick all its own for getting these seeds scattered. Plants have a great number of clever tricks to this end, but few of them copy the Hevea. When its seeds are dry and ready to hunt a place to start a new plant, the pod explodes. It may throw the seeds forty to fifty feet.

The Hevea is a tree of moderate height, found in the natural state scattered here and there through dense forests. It does not branch near the ground. It has three leaves on a stem, something like locust leaves. It sheds these every year, but, being a tropical tree, it does this a few at a time, so that it is always well supplied with leaves.

As the need of rubber grew, it was supplied chiefly from Brazil. The demand for rubber sent more and more natives into the forests. There they worked by a method of their own. A native would literally cut out a job for himself. He would do this by cutting a trail that would wander through the jungle from one rubber tree to another. These trees were scattered and the trail might be three miles long before it came out of the woods at the same place it had entered. The native who had cut the trail would then set himself to the task of visiting each of his trees every day and collecting the juice that had dripped from the gashes he had cut into it the day before.

The juice of the rubber tree is called *latex*. It is not sap like the sirup that comes from the maple-sugar tree. It flows in channels that are different from those in which the sap flows.

The fig tree belongs to a family that produces this latex and yields rubber. Break a twig off a fig tree, and a white liquid will appear. This liquid is rubber in the raw.

Nobody seems to know why rubber trees produce this latex. It looks very much like milk. Strangely, it acts like milk. Let it stand and the rubber will rise to the top as cream rises on milk. Put certain chemicals in it and the rubber in it will curdle as milk curdles.

RUBBER TAPPER AT WORK

When the native gets back to camp with his milk of the rubber tree, he has his own way of changing it into the form of rubber. He builds a smoky fire. He dips a broad paddle into the latex, which sticks to it like molasses. He turns the paddle about in the smoke of the fire and the latex hardens. He dips the paddle again, hardens its coating again, and thus puts on another layer of rubber. He keeps this up until he has a piece that might weigh twenty pounds. He cuts it off his paddle and it is rubber ready to start to market. It takes the journey down the Amazon and enters the market as Para rubber.

Rubber taken in this way from trees that grow in their native forests is called *wild* rubber. There was quite enough of it to supply the demand for rubber a generation ago. That was before the time of the automobile, which has come to use the bulk of the rubber of the world for tires.

The demand for rubber made by the automobile was quite sudden. It did not exist in 1900. By 1915 it was in full swing. About 30,000 tons of wild rubber were being produced every year. In a little while automobiles alone were demanding hundreds of thousands of tons. If automobile manufacturers could not have secured that amount of rubber, they could not have gone on producing automobiles as we know them. It would have been impossible to meet the demand with wild rubber.

A most fortunate incident happened nearly half a century earlier and this incident saved the situation. An Englishman named Henry Wickham had studied rubber along the Amazon. He came to a very important conclusion. He thought that these rubber trees could be planted on plantations and that rubber might be grown as a cultivated crop. He believed that they could be grown in India, which was controlled by the British. He convinced the Director of Kew Gardens, in London, that it would be a fine thing if India could be interested in developing rubber plantations. India was, in fact, interested.

The seeds of the rubber tree must be handled very carefully and not held too long or the spark of life in them dies and they will not sprout. Henry Wickham worried for a long time about a way to get these seeds quickly to Kew Gardens, where they could be grown into small plants and then sent on to India. He was high up the Amazon River and there were few ships leaving for England. But fortune favored him. A lonesome steamer came up the great river, but failed to get a return cargo. There was no money to run it any further and it was abandoned. Wickham chartered this ship, got his rubber seed aboard, and hurried at top speed to London.

A good many of the seeds grew. The next year the little rubber trees were sent to India. They were not well received. India had lost interest in them. They were taken on to Ceylon, which is the island at the tip end of India, and some of them were planted there. Others were carried on to the Malay Peninsula, which is beyond India. More of them were planted there than anywhere else. Singapore is the seaport city at the end of the Malay Peninsula. The little slips were planted in the botanic gardens at Singapore and grew to be fine trees. Nobody, however, seemed interested in developing rubber plantations.

A great deal of coffee was grown in this part of the world. About the time that the rubber trees were grown and were producing many seeds, the coffee crop failed. The coffee plants got a disease which killed them. The coffee planters were looking around for some other crop to which they might turn. The demand for rubber was increasing, because it was needed for making tires for bicycles which were then popular. Nobody then dreamed of the automobile which was soon to appear and demand

TAPPING A RUBBER TREE IN HONDURAS

always more and more rubber. Many plantations were developed, however, and many planters learned how to grow and care for rubber trees. They were ready to expand their plantings when the great demand came. It grew as the automobile came into use. The amount of plantation rubber that was used came to be many times greater than that of wild rubber. A huge industry was developed in the tropical Far East. Singapore came to be its center.

Thus the Hevea tree of Brazil came to be a cultivated crop. When the World War was over, the manufacturers of automobiles in America began to look around for other sources of rubber than the Far East. The American tropics, the Philippines, many lands other than those around Singapore, were good places for rubber plantations. Soon rubber began to promise that it would come to be a crop cultivated in many lands. So rapidly were its uses increasing, however, that this did not threaten the old plantations of the East. Planters there were ripe in experience and well able to meet all competition.

It is usually a dense jungle that is selected for a rubber plantation. This tropical tree will grow well where other tropical trees have been growing. There must be much rainfall all through the year. It is no easy task to clear up the jungle and get it ready for planting. Young trees from the nursery that are a year old and six or seven feet high are set out. Then the other growth must be kept down while they are getting started. When they are five or six years old, they are ready to begin to yield a bit in return for the labor that has been spent on them.

Tapping the trees to get the latex is very much more skilfully done on the plantations than in the Amazon forests. First a channel is cut in the bark, straight down the side of the tree. This is to be used as a drain for the latex that is to come in from the sides. A cup is placed beneath it to catch the dripping fluid. Then the native tapper, who becomes very skilful, cuts a gash which may run one fourth of the way around the tree and which will drain into the main channel. It must be cut just deep enough to reach the latex but not deep enough to cut off the flow of the sap. When this gash is cut, the latex begins to flow. It may flow for but a half hour and stop. The next day the tapper will come back and collect the milk. He will shave a thin slice off the lower edge of this gash. This opens the cells and starts the flow of latex all over again.

Day after day, month after month, year after year, the rubber tree on the plantation is thus cut, that it may give up its mite of latex. More rubber trees on more plantations are being mustered into this service every year. The juice that they secrete goes through one process after another that advances it along the road of development. It furnishes employment for hundreds of thousands of people in many lands. Its care is rapidly becoming one of the large and vital industries of the world. The products that result are important to every member of every civilized community in the world.

Who has not noted the cushioned ease with which the automobile rolls along on its balloon tires? This is only one plain example of the results that have come from man's study of the juice of a tree from which American Indians long ago made strange balls that would bounce. It is the contribution of a single plant to the progress of the world.

INDEX

A CATALOGUE OF SELECTED DOVER BOOKS
IN ALL FIELDS OF INTEREST

A CATALOGUE OF SELECTED DOVER BOOKS IN ALL FIELDS OF INTEREST

WHAT IS SCIENCE?, *N. Campbell*

The role of experiment and measurement, the function of mathematics, the nature of scientific laws, the difference between laws and theories, the limitations of science, and many similarly provocative topics are treated clearly and without technicalities by an eminent scientist. "Still an excellent introduction to scientific philosophy," H. Margenau in *Physics Today*. "A first-rate primer . . . deserves a wide audience," *Scientific American*. 192pp. 5⅜ x 8.
S43 Paperbound $1.25

THE NATURE OF LIGHT AND COLOUR IN THE OPEN AIR, *M. Minnaert*

Why are shadows sometimes blue, sometimes green, or other colors depending on the light and surroundings? What causes mirages? Why do multiple suns and moons appear in the sky? Professor Minnaert explains these unusual phenomena and hundreds of others in simple, easy-to-understand terms based on optical laws and the properties of light and color. No mathematics is required but artists, scientists, students, and everyone fascinated by these "tricks" of nature will find thousands of useful and amazing pieces of information. Hundreds of observational experiments are suggested which require no special equipment. 200 illustrations; 42 photos. xvi + 362pp. 5⅜ x 8.
T196 Paperbound $2.00

THE STRANGE STORY OF THE QUANTUM, AN ACCOUNT FOR THE GENERAL READER OF THE GROWTH OF IDEAS UNDERLYING OUR PRESENT ATOMIC KNOWLEDGE, *B. Hoffmann*

Presents lucidly and expertly, with barest amount of mathematics, the problems and theories which led to modern quantum physics. Dr. Hoffmann begins with the closing years of the 19th century, when certain trifling discrepancies were noticed, and with illuminating analogies and examples takes you through the brilliant concepts of Planck, Einstein, Pauli, Broglie, Bohr, Schroedinger, Heisenberg, Dirac, Sommerfeld, Feynman, etc. This edition includes a new, long postscript carrying the story through 1958. "Of the books attempting an account of the history and contents of our modern atomic physics which have come to my attention, this is the best," H. Margenau, Yale University, in *American Journal of Physics*. 32 tables and line illustrations. Index. 275pp. 5⅜ x 8.
T518 Paperbound $2.00

GREAT IDEAS OF MODERN MATHEMATICS: THEIR NATURE AND USE, *Jagjit Singh*

Reader with only high school math will understand main mathematical ideas of modern physics, astronomy, genetics, psychology, evolution, etc. better than many who use them as tools, but comprehend little of their basic structure. Author uses his wide knowledge of non-mathematical fields in brilliant exposition of differential equations, matrices, group theory, logic, statistics, problems of mathematical foundations, imaginary numbers, vectors, etc. Original publication. 2 appendixes. 2 indexes. 65 ills. 322pp. 5⅜ x 8.
T587 Paperbound $2.00

A SHORT ACCOUNT OF THE HISTORY OF MATHEMATICS, *W. W. Rouse Ball*

Last previous edition (1908) hailed by mathematicians and laymen for lucid overview of math as living science, for understandable presentation of individual contributions of great mathematicians. Treats lives, discoveries of every important school and figure from Egypt, Phoenicia to late nineteenth century. Greek schools of Ionia, Cyzicus, Alexandria, Byzantium, Pythagoras; primitive arithmetic; Middle Ages and Renaissance, including European and Asiatic contributions; modern math of Descartes, Pascal, Wallis, Huygens, Newton, Euler, Lambert, Laplace, scores more. More emphasis on historical development, exposition of ideas than other books on subject. Non-technical, readable text can be followed with no more preparation than high-school algebra. Index. 544pp. 5⅜ x 8. Paperbound $2.25

GREAT IDEAS AND THEORIES OF MODERN COSMOLOGY, *Jagjit Singh*

Companion volume to author's popular "Great Ideas of Modern Mathematics" (Dover, $2.00). The best non-technical survey of post-Einstein attempts to answer perhaps unanswerable questions of origin, age of Universe, possibility of life on other worlds, etc. Fundamental theories of cosmology and cosmogony recounted, explained, evaluated in light of most recent data: Einstein's concepts of relativity, space-time; Milne's a priori world-system; astrophysical theories of Jeans, Eddington; Hoyle's "continuous creation;" contributions of dozens more scientists. A faithful, comprehensive critical summary of complex material presented in an extremely well-written text intended for laymen. Original publication. Index. xii + 276pp. 5⅜ x 8½. Paperbound $2.00

THE RESTLESS UNIVERSE, *Max Born*

A remarkably lucid account by a Nobel Laureate of recent theories of wave mechanics, behavior of gases, electrons and ions, waves and particles, electronic structure of the atom, nuclear physics, and similar topics. "Much more thorough and deeper than most attempts . . . easy and delightful," *Chemical and Engineering News*. Special feature: 7 animated sequences of 60 figures each showing such phenomena as gas molecules in motion, the scattering of alpha particles, etc. 11 full-page plates of photographs. Total of nearly 600 illustrations. 351pp. 6⅛ x 9¼. Paperbound $2.00

PLANETS, STARS AND GALAXIES: DESCRIPTIVE ASTRONOMY FOR BEGINNERS, *A. E. Fanning*

What causes the progression of the seasons? Phases of the moon? The Aurora Borealis? How much does the sun weigh? What are the chances of life on our sister planets? Absorbing introduction to astronomy, incorporating the latest discoveries and theories: the solar wind, the surface temperature of Venus, the pock-marked face of Mars, quasars, and much more. Places you on the frontiers of one of the most vital sciences of our time. Revised (1966). Introduction by Donald H. Menzel, Harvard University. References. Index. 45 illustrations. 189pp. 5¼ x 8¼. Paperbound $1.50

GREAT IDEAS IN INFORMATION THEORY, LANGUAGE AND CYBERNETICS, *Jagjit Singh*

Non-mathematical, but profound study of information, language, the codes used by men and machines to communicate, the principles of analog and digital computers, work of McCulloch, Pitts, von Neumann, Turing, and Uttley, correspondences between intricate mechanical network of "thinking machines" and more intricate neurophysiological mechanism of human brain. Indexes. 118 figures. 50 tables. ix + 338pp. 5⅜ x 8½. Paperbound $2.00

THE MUSIC OF THE SPHERES: THE MATERIAL UNIVERSE—FROM ATOM TO QUASAR, SIMPLY EXPLAINED, *Guy Murchie*
Vast compendium of fact, modern concept and theory, observed and calculated data, historical background guides intelligent layman through the material universe. Brilliant exposition of earth's construction, explanations for moon's craters, atmospheric components of Venus and Mars (with data from recent fly-by's), sun spots, sequences of star birth and death, neighboring galaxies, contributions of Galileo, Tycho Brahe, Kepler, etc.; and (Vol. 2) construction of the atom (describing newly discovered sigma and xi subatomic particles), theories of sound, color and light, space and time, including relativity theory, quantum theory, wave theory, probability theory, work of Newton, Maxwell, Faraday, Einstein, de Broglie, etc. "Best presentation yet offered to the intelligent general reader," *Saturday Review*. Revised (1967). Index. 319 illustrations by the author. Total of xx + 644pp. 5⅜ x 8½.
Vol. 1 Paperbound $2.00, Vol. 2 Paperbound $2.00,
The set $4.00

FOUR LECTURES ON RELATIVITY AND SPACE, *Charles Proteus Steinmetz*
Lecture series, given by great mathematician and electrical engineer, generally considered one of the best popular-level expositions of special and general relativity theories and related questions. Steinmetz translates complex mathematical reasoning into language accessible to laymen through analogy, example and comparison. Among topics covered are relativity of motion, location, time; of mass; acceleration; 4-dimensional time-space; geometry of the gravitational field; curvature and bending of space; non-Euclidean geometry. Index. 40 illustrations. x + 142pp. 5⅜ x 8½. Paperbound $1.35

HOW TO KNOW THE WILD FLOWERS, *Mrs. William Starr Dana*
Classic nature book that has introduced thousands to wonders of American wild flowers. Color-season principle of organization is easy to use, even by those with no botanical training, and the genial, refreshing discussions of history, folklore, uses of over 1,000 native and escape flowers, foliage plants are informative as well as fun to read. Over 170 full-page plates, collected from several editions, may be colored in to make permanent records of finds. Revised to conform with 1950 edition of Gray's Manual of Botany. xlii + 438pp. 5⅜ x 8½. Paperbound $2.00

MANUAL OF THE TREES OF NORTH AMERICA, *Charles Sprague Sargent*
Still unsurpassed as most comprehensive, reliable study of North American tree characteristics, precise locations and distribution. By dean of American dendrologists. Every tree native to U.S., Canada, Alaska; 185 genera, 717 species, described in detail—leaves, flowers, fruit, winterbuds, bark, wood, growth habits, etc. plus discussion of varieties and local variants, immaturity variations. Over 100 keys, including unusual 11-page analytical key to genera, aid in identification. 783 clear illustrations of flowers, fruit, leaves. An unmatched permanent reference work for all nature lovers. Second enlarged (1926) edition. Synopsis of families. Analytical key to genera. Glossary of technical terms. Index. 783 illustrations, 1 map. Total of 982pp. 5⅜ x 8.
Vol. 1 Paperbound $2.25, Vol. 2 Paperbound $2.25,
The set $4.50

IT'S FUN TO MAKE THINGS FROM SCRAP MATERIALS, *Evelyn Glantz Hershoff*
What use are empty spools, tin cans, bottle tops? What can be made from rubber bands, clothes pins, paper clips, and buttons? This book provides simply worded instructions and large diagrams showing you how to make cookie cutters, toy trucks, paper turkeys, Halloween masks, telephone sets, aprons, linoleum block- and spatter prints — in all 399 projects! Many are easy enough for young children to figure out for themselves; some challenging enough to entertain adults; all are remarkably ingenious ways to make things from materials that cost pennies or less! Formerly "Scrap Fun for Everyone." Index. 214 illustrations. 373pp. 5⅜ x 8½. Paperbound $1.50

SYMBOLIC LOGIC and THE GAME OF LOGIC, *Lewis Carroll*
"Symbolic Logic" is not concerned with modern symbolic logic, but is instead a collection of over 380 problems posed with charm and imagination, using the syllogism and a fascinating diagrammatic method of drawing conclusions. In "The Game of Logic" Carroll's whimsical imagination devises a logical game played with 2 diagrams and counters (included) to manipulate hundreds of tricky syllogisms. The final section, "Hit or Miss" is a lagniappe of 101 additional puzzles in the delightful Carroll manner. Until this reprint edition, both of these books were rarities costing up to $15 each. Symbolic Logic: Index. xxxi + 199pp. The Game of Logic: 96pp. 2 vols. bound as one. 5⅜ x 8. Paperbound $2.00

MATHEMATICAL PUZZLES OF SAM LOYD, PART I
selected and edited by M. Gardner
Choice puzzles by the greatest American puzzle creator and innovator. Selected from his famous collection, "Cyclopedia of Puzzles," they retain the unique style and historical flavor of the originals. There are posers based on arithmetic, algebra, probability, game theory, route tracing, topology, counter and sliding block, operations research, geometrical dissection. Includes the famous "14-15" puzzle which was a national craze, and his "Horse of a Different Color" which sold millions of copies. 117 of his most ingenious puzzles in all. 120 line drawings and diagrams. Solutions. Selected references. xx + 167pp. 5⅜ x 8. Paperbound $1.00

STRING FIGURES AND HOW TO MAKE THEM, *Caroline Furness Jayne*
107 string figures plus variations selected from the best primitive and modern examples developed by Navajo, Apache, pygmies of Africa, Eskimo, in Europe, Australia, China, etc. The most readily understandable, easy-to-follow book in English on perennially popular recreation. Crystal-clear exposition; step-by-step diagrams. Everyone from kindergarten children to adults looking for unusual diversion will be endlessly amused. Index. Bibliography. Introduction by A. C. Haddon. 17 full-page plates, 960 illustrations. xxiii + 401pp. 5⅜ x 8½. Paperbound $2.00

PAPER FOLDING FOR BEGINNERS, *W. D. Murray and F. J. Rigney*
A delightful introduction to the varied and entertaining Japanese art of origami (paper folding), with a full, crystal-clear text that anticipates every difficulty; over 275 clearly labeled diagrams of all important stages in creation. You get results at each stage, since complex figures are logically developed from simpler ones. 43 different pieces are explained: sailboats, frogs, roosters, etc. 6 photographic plates. 279 diagrams. 95pp. 5⅝ x 8⅜. Paperbound $1.00

PRINCIPLES OF ART HISTORY,
H. Wölfflin
Analyzing such terms as "baroque," "classic," "neoclassic," "primitive," "picturesque," and 164 different works by artists like Botticelli, van Cleve, Dürer, Hobbema, Holbein, Hals, Rembrandt, Titian, Brueghel, Vermeer, and many others, the author establishes the classifications of art history and style on a firm, concrete basis. This classic of art criticism shows what really occurred between the 14th-century primitives and the sophistication of the 18th century in terms of basic attitudes and philosophies. "A remarkable lesson in the art of seeing," *Sat. Rev. of Literature.* Translated from the 7th German edition. 150 illustrations. 254pp. 6⅛ x 9¼. Paperbound $2.00

PRIMITIVE ART,
Franz Boas
This authoritative and exhaustive work by a great American anthropologist covers the entire gamut of primitive art. Pottery, leatherwork, metal work, stone work, wood, basketry, are treated in detail. Theories of primitive art, historical depth in art history, technical virtuosity, unconscious levels of patterning, symbolism, styles, literature, music, dance, etc. A must book for the interested layman, the anthropologist, artist, handicrafter (hundreds of unusual motifs), and the historian. Over 900 illustrations (50 ceramic vessels, 12 totem poles, etc.). 376pp. 5⅜ x 8. Paperbound $2.25

THE GENTLEMAN AND CABINET MAKER'S DIRECTOR,
Thomas Chippendale
A reprint of the 1762 catalogue of furniture designs that went on to influence generations of English and Colonial and Early Republic American furniture makers. The 200 plates, most of them full-page sized, show Chippendale's designs for French (Louis XV), Gothic, and Chinese-manner chairs, sofas, canopy and dome beds, cornices, chamber organs, cabinets, shaving tables, commodes, picture frames, frets, candle stands, chimney pieces, decorations, etc. The drawings are all elegant and highly detailed; many include construction diagrams and elevations. A supplement of 24 photographs shows surviving pieces of original and Chippendale-style pieces of furniture. Brief biography of Chippendale by N. I. Bienenstock, editor of *Furniture World.* Reproduced from the 1762 edition. 200 plates, plus 19 photographic plates. vi + 249pp. 9⅛ x 12¼. Paperbound $3.50

AMERICAN ANTIQUE FURNITURE: A BOOK FOR AMATEURS,
Edgar G. Miller, Jr.
Standard introduction and practical guide to identification of valuable American antique furniture. 2115 illustrations, mostly photographs taken by the author in 148 private homes, are arranged in chronological order in extensive chapters on chairs, sofas, chests, desks, bedsteads, mirrors, tables, clocks, and other articles. Focus is on furniture accessible to the collector, including simpler pieces and a larger than usual coverage of Empire style. Introductory chapters identify structural elements, characteristics of various styles, how to avoid fakes, etc. "We are frequently asked to name some book on American furniture that will meet the requirements of the novice collector, the beginning dealer, and . . . the general public. . . . We believe Mr. Miller's two volumes more completely satisfy this specification than any other work," *Antiques.* Appendix. Index. Total of vi + 1106pp. 7⅞ x 10¾.
Two volume set, paperbound $7.50

TREES OF THE EASTERN AND CENTRAL UNITED STATES AND CANADA, *W. M. Harlow*
A revised edition of a standard middle-level guide to native trees and important escapes. More than 140 trees are described in detail, and illustrated with more than 600 drawings and photographs. Supplementary keys will enable the careful reader to identify almost any tree he might encounter. xiii + 288pp. 5⅜ x 8. Paperbound $1.45

INSECT LIFE AND INSECT NATURAL HISTORY, *S. W. Frost*
A work emphasizing habits, social life, and ecological relations of insects, rather than more academic aspects of classification and morphology. Prof. Frost's enthusiasm and knowledge are everywhere evident as he discusses insect associations and specialized habits like leaf-rolling, leaf-mining, and case-making, the gall insects, the boring insects, aquatic insects, etc. He examines all sorts of matters not usually covered in general works such as: insects as human food, insect music and musicians, insect response to electric and radio waves, use of insects in art and literature. The admirably executed purpose of this book, which covers the middle ground between elementary treatment and scholarly monographs, is to excite the reader to observe for himself. Over 700 illustrations. Extensive bibliography. x + 542pp. 5⅜ x 8. Paperbound $2.50

HANDBOOK OF BIRDS OF EASTERN NORTH AMERICA, *Frank M. Chapman*
Formerly *the* field guide to Eastern birds. Still contains most complete descriptions of plumages, behavior, nest and eggs, habitat, etc. as observed in the field by Chapman and other important ornithologists. Generally, the most comprehensive compendium of bird lore available in the handbook format. Color keys. Illustrated synopsis of orders and suborders. Index. 195 illustrations. xxxvi + 581pp. 5⅜ x 8½. Paperbound $3.25

LIFE HISTORIES OF NORTH AMERICAN BIRDS, *Arthur Cleveland Bent*
Monumental series of books on North American birds, prepared and published under auspices of Smithsonian Institution. The definitive coverage of the subject; the most-used single source of information. Entire 22-volume set now available from Dover in inexpensive paperbound format. An encyclopedic collection of detailed, specific observations utilizing reports of hundreds of contemporary observers, writings of such naturalists as Audubon, Burroughs, William Brewster, as well as author's own extensive investigations. Contains literally everything known about life history of each bird considered (over 1160 species): nesting, eggs, plumage, distribution and migration, voice, enemies, courtship display, etc. Each volume fully illustrated with up to 393 photographs. 22-volume complete set, Paperbound $59.95

Prices subject to change without notice.

Available at your book dealer or write for free catalogue to Dept. Adsci, Dover Publications, Inc., 180 Varick St., N.Y., N.Y. 10014. Dover publishes more than 150 books each year on science, elementary and advanced mathematics, biology, music, art, literary history, social sciences and other areas.